A Light in the Clouds

THE AZRIELI SERIES OF HOLOCAUST SURVIVOR MEMOIRS: PUBLISHED TITLES

ENGLISH TITLES

Zuzana Sermer, *Survival Kit*

Rachel Shtibel, *The Violin*/ Adam Shtibel,
  A Child's Testimony

Maxwell Smart, *Chaos to Canvas*

Gerta Solan, *My Heart Is At Ease*

Zsuzsanna Fischer Spiro, *In Fragile
  Moments*/ Eva Shainblum, *The Last Time*

George Stern, *Vanished Boyhood*

Willie Sterner, *The Shadows Behind Me*

Ann Szedlecki, *Album of My Life*

William Tannenzapf, *Memories from the
  Abyss*/ Renate Krakauer, *But I Had a
  Happy Childhood*

Elsa Thon, *If Only It Were Fiction*

Agnes Tomasov, *From Generation to Generation*

Joseph Tomasov, *From Loss to Liberation*

Leslie Vertes, *Alone in the Storm*

Anka Voticky, *Knocking on Every Door*

Sam Weisberg, *Carry the Torch*/ Johnny
  Jablon, *A Lasting Legacy*

TITRES FRANÇAIS

Judy Abrams, *Retenue par un fil*/ Eva Felsen-
  burg Marx, *Une question de chance*

Molly Applebaum, *Les Mots enfouis: Le
  Journal de Molly Applebaum*

Claire Baum, *Le Colis caché*

Bronia et Joseph Beker, *Plus forts que le
  malheur*

Max Bornstein, *Citoyen de nulle part*

Tommy Dick, *Objectif: survivre*

Marian Domanski, *Traqué*

John Freund, *La Fin du printemps*

Myrna Goldenberg (Éditrice), *Un combat
  singulier: Femmes dans la tourmente de
  l'Holocauste*

René Goldman, *Une enfance à la dérive*

Pinchas Gutter, *Dans la chambre noire*

Anna Molnár Hegedűs, *Pendant la saison
  des lilas*

Helena Jockel, *Nous chantions en sourdine*

Michael Kutz, *Si, par miracle*

Nate Leipciger, *Le Poids de la liberté*

Alex Levin, *Étoile jaune, étoile rouge*

Fred Mann, *Un terrible revers de fortune*

Michael Mason, *Au fil d'un nom*

Leslie Meisels, *Soudain, les ténèbres*

Muguette Myers, *Les Lieux du courage*

Arthur Ney, *L'Heure W*

Felix Opatowski, *L'Antichambre de l'enfer*

Marguerite Élias Quddus, *Cachée*

Henia Reinhartz, *Fragments de ma vie*

Betty Rich, *Seule au monde*

Paul-Henri Rips, *Matricule E/96*

Steve Rotschild, *Sur les traces du passé*

Kitty Salsberg et Ellen Foster, *Unies dans
  l'épreuve*

Zuzana Sermer, *Trousse de survie*

Rachel Shtibel, *Le Violon*/ Adam Shtibel,
  Témoignage d'un enfant

George Stern, *Une jeunesse perdue*

Willie Sterner, *Les Ombres du passé*

Ann Szedlecki, *L'Album de ma vie*

William Tannenzapf, *Souvenirs de l'abîme*/
  Renate Krakauer, *Le Bonheur de
  l'innocence*

Elsa Thon, *Que renaisse demain*

Agnes Tomasov, *De génération en génération*

Leslie Vertes, *Seul dans la tourmente*

Anka Voticky, *Frapper à toutes les portes*

Sam Weisberg, *Passeur de mémoire*/
  Johnny Jablon, *Souvenez-vous*

A Light in the Clouds
Margalith Esterhuizen

THE AZRIELI FOUNDATION · www.azrielifoundation.org

Cover design by Endpaper Studio
Cover photo by Chris Nguyen on Unsplash
Book design by Mark Goldstein
Interior map by Deborah Crowle
Endpaper maps by Martin Gilbert

LIBRARY AND ARCHIVES CANADA CATALOGUING IN PUBLICATION

A light in the clouds/ Margalith Esterhuizen.
    Esterhuizen, Margalith, 1927– , author. Azrieli Foundation, publisher.
The Azrieli series of Holocaust survivor memoirs; XIV
Includes bibliographical references and index.
Canadiana 20220212791 · ISBN 9781989719312 (softcover)
LCSH: Esterhuizen, Margalith, 1927– · LCSH: Jews — Romania — Rădăuți — Biography. · LCSH: Jewish children in the Holocaust — Romania — Biography. · LCSH: Holocaust survivors — Romania — Biography. · LCSH: Holocaust, Jewish (1939–1945) — Romania — Personal narratives. · LCGFT: Autobiographies.

LCC DS135.R73 E88 2022 · DDC 940.53/18092 — DC23

PRINTED IN CANADA

The Azrieli Foundation's Holocaust Survivor Memoirs Program

Naomi Azrieli, Publisher

Jody Spiegel, Program Director
Arielle Berger, Managing Editor
Catherine Person, Manager and Editor of French Translations
Catherine Aubé, Editor of French Translations
Matt Carrington, Editor
Devora Levin, Editor and Special Projects Coordinator
Stephanie Corazza, Historian and Manager of Academic Initiatives
Marc-Olivier Cloutier, Manager of Education Initiatives
Nadine Auclair, Coordinator of Education Initiatives
Michelle Sadowski, Educator
Elin Beaumont, Community and Education Initiatives
Elizabeth Banks, Digital Asset Curator and Archivist

Mark Goldstein, Art Director
Bruno Paradis, Layout, French-Language Editions

Contents

Series Preface: In their own words...

In telling these stories, the writers have liberated themselves. For so many years we did not speak about it, even when we became free people living in a free society. Now, when at last we are writing about what happened to us in this dark period of history, knowing that our stories will be read and live on, it is possible for us to feel truly free. These unique historical documents put a face on what was lost, and allow readers to grasp the enormity of what happened to six million Jews — one story at a time.

David J. Azrieli, C.M., C.Q., M.Arch
Holocaust survivor and founder, The Azrieli Foundation

Since the end of World War II, approximately 40,000 Jewish Holocaust survivors have immigrated to Canada. Who they are, where they came from, what they experienced and how they built new lives for themselves and their families are important parts of our Canadian heritage. The Azrieli Foundation's Holocaust Survivor Memoirs Program was established in 2005 to preserve and share the memoirs written by those who survived the twentieth-century Nazi genocide of the Jews of Europe and later made their way to Canada. The memoirs encourage readers to engage thoughtfully and critically with the complexities of the Holocaust and to create meaningful connections with the lives of survivors.

Millions of individual stories are lost to us forever. By preserving the stories written by survivors and making them widely available to a broad audience, the Azrieli Foundation's Holocaust Survivor Memoirs Program seeks to sustain the memory of all those who perished at the hands of hatred, abetted by indifference and apathy. The personal accounts of those who survived against all odds are as different as the people who wrote them, but all demonstrate the courage, strength, wit and luck that it took to prevail and survive in such terrible adversity. The memoirs are also moving tributes to people — strangers and friends — who risked their lives to help others, and who, through acts of kindness and decency in the darkest of moments, frequently helped the persecuted maintain faith in humanity and courage to endure. These accounts offer inspiration to all, as does the survivors' desire to share their experiences so that new generations can learn from them.

The Holocaust Survivor Memoirs Program collects, archives and publishes select survivor memoirs and makes the print editions available free of charge to educational institutions and Holocaust-education programs across Canada. They are also available for sale online to the general public. All revenues to the Azrieli Foundation from the sales of the Azrieli Series of Holocaust Survivor Memoirs go toward the publishing and educational work of the memoirs program.

⌇

The Azrieli Foundation would like to express appreciation to the following people for their invaluable efforts in producing this book: Doris Bergen, Judith Clark, Diana Dumitru, Mark Duffus (Maracle Inc.), Gaëlle Fisher, Alison Strobel, and the team at Second Story Press.

Editorial Note

The following memoir contains terms, concepts and historical references that may be unfamiliar to the reader. English translations of foreign-language words and terms have been added to the text, and parentheses have been used to include the names and locations of present-day towns and cities when place names have changed. The editors of this memoir have worked to maintain the author's voice and stay true to the original narrative while maintaining historical accuracy. General information on major organizations, significant historical events and people, geographical locations, religious and cultural terms, and foreign-language words and expressions that will help give context to the events described in the text can be found in the glossary beginning on page 67.

Introduction

The northeastern borderlands of Romania, where Margalith Esterhuizen was born and spent her childhood, occupy a complex place
in Jewish history and memory. Early-twentieth-century Czernowitz
(later Romanian Cernăuți; now known as Chernivtsi in contemporary
Ukraine), for example, the capital of the historical region of Bukovina,
calls to mind a confident, well-established, mostly German-speaking
Jewish community. Representing over a third of the population, Jews
in this city developed a vibrant culture and strong regional identity.
Even after the end of World War II, many exiled Jewish Bukovinians
continued to praise the character of this area, which was shaped by
its having belonged to the Habsburg Empire for 150 years, its unique
cultural diversity and favourable natural features.[1]

Meanwhile, Kishinev (now known as Chișinău in contemporary
Moldova) in historical Bessarabia, a city situated on equally fertile
land where almost half of the inhabitants were Jewish at the turn of
the twentieth century, was also a major centre of Jewish — specifically Yiddish — culture and literature. However, Kishinev is now mostly

---

1 On this, see Marianne Hirsch and Leo Spitzer, *Ghosts of Home: The Afterlife of
Czernowitz in Jewish Memory* (Berkeley: University of California Press, 2010);
Gaëlle Fisher, *Resettlers and Survivors: Bukovina and the Politics of Belonging in
West Germany and Israel, 1945–1989* (New York: Berghahn, 2020).

identified with the bloody pogrom that took place there in 1903 when the area was still under Tsarist Russian rule. In this region, in the early twentieth century, antisemitism grew especially virulent.[2] Then, during World War II, both Bessarabia and Bukovina became key locations of the Holocaust in Romania — a still little-known but infamous chapter of the persecution of European Jews, which resulted in the estimated murder of between 280,000 and 380,000 people.[3]

The borderlands of Romania thus belong in equal measure on a map of the Holocaust and a map of European Jewish culture. The particular significance of Margalith Esterhuizen's memoir, therefore, is not only what it adds to our understanding of the social processes and conditions that led to the mass murder of European Jews: as an emotional, highly personal and sensory account, written from the perspective of a child but also from the perspective of an older person looking back at her life after many decades, this memoir opens new vistas and offers new insights into the history and the legacies of persecution alike. It also adds to our knowledge of the interwoven and rich social fabrics that existed and were then largely destroyed, and testifies to how this past continues to reverberate and resonate today around the world.

Margalith Esterhuizen (née Herscovici) was born in 1927 in Rădăuţi — a small town in southern Bukovina in northern Romania, where her mother, Rachel Maimon, was from. Her father, Moritz Srul Herscovici, hailed from Herţa (now Hertsa, Ukraine), a small town some thirty kilometres farther east, close to the border with

---

2 See Diana Dumitru, *The State, Antisemitism, and Collaboration: The Borderlands of Romania and the Soviet Union* (New York: Cambridge University Press, 2016).

3 For this estimate and a concise but detailed account of the Holocaust in Romania, see Tuvia Friling et al., *International Commission on the Holocaust in Romania: Final Report* (Bucharest: Polirom, 2004). See also Radu Ioanid, *The Holocaust in Romania: The Destruction of Jews and Gypsies under the Antonescu Regime, 1940–1944* (Chicago: Ivan R. Dee, 2000).

Bessarabia. The family later moved to Cernăuți in northern Bukovina and then Edineți in northern Bessarabia (now Edineț in the Republic of Moldova). Margalith was familiar with Jewish traditions and religious practices, through her grandparents and extended family, especially on her father's side, and though she does not specify this, her native language is likely to have been Yiddish. However, the world she was born into was distinctly multilingual and multiethnic. At the time of her birth, in Bukovina and Bessarabia, Jews represented only 12 per cent and 7.2 per cent of the overall population, respectively. In Rădăuți, in the early twentieth century, more than half of the population's native language was German or Yiddish, and the other half spoke Romanian as well as some Russian, Ukrainian and Polish. In Bessarabia, too, most Jews spoke Yiddish or German; however, like the rest of the population, many also spoke Russian or, in some cases, Romanian. While it is true that in this part of Europe ethnicity, occupation and class tended to overlap, the Jewish and non-Jewish worlds intertwined in many and complex ways. Margalith does not engage with this directly in her memoir. But the fact that for some time she attended a Catholic school run by German nuns and the ease with which her family moved across the region testify to the degree of interethnic mingling and her own degree of acculturation.

Like many other Jewish memoirists of her generation, Margalith describes a happy childhood. But there is no doubt that the dramatic changes and political upheaval Bukovina and Bessarabia experienced over the course of the early twentieth century had huge consequences for social realities in these areas and the lives of Jews in particular. Integrated into Romania following the collapse of the Austro-Hungarian and Russian empires at the end of World War I, the areas and their inhabitants subsequently underwent a process of "Romanianization" — the Romanian brand of nationalization. The changes were not just territorial and political but economic, social and cultural. They included the imposition of the Romanian language in schools, universities and state institutions and banning the use of other languages in public; the dismissal or exclusion of alleged "foreigners" from government positions and important sectors of the economy; and policies of systematic discrimination that led to the large-scale alienation and pauperization of specific social groups.[4]

Although Romanianization affected all "non-Romanians," the main target of these measures was Jews. The Romanian constitution of 1923 was supposed to have provided for Jews' full emancipation, and the "Minorities Treaties" agreed upon in Paris in 1919 were meant to guarantee the protection of the rights of so-called national minorities, including Jews. But in Romania, these agreements were flouted from the outset, and efforts to disenfranchise Jews, together with political and popular antisemitism, grew in intensity during the interwar period. By the late 1930s, the Iron Guard, a homegrown fascist movement, was one of the largest political forces in Romania, and antisemitism was at the forefront of political life. In the face of this, the state displayed what Diana Dumitru has described as "a criminal level of complacency."[5] By 1938, the king, Carol II, had turned to authoritarianism, and some 200,000 Jews — mostly from the borderlands — had been stripped of their citizenship. In the preceding years, many Jews had left the country, mostly for Palestine; however, for those who remained as war approached, like for Jews in the rest of Europe, emigration proved increasingly unrealistic and difficult.

With the outbreak of World War II in September 1939, Jews in the borderlands of Romania felt the entrapment and the effects of the geopolitical contest over their homelands in an especially drastic manner. The first major event was the sudden Soviet invasion of

---

4 For an overview of the situation in interwar Romania, see Ezra Mendelsohn, *The Jews of East Central Europe between the World Wars* (Bloomington: Indiana University Press, 1993), 170–211; Liviu Rotman and Raphael Vago, eds., *The History of the Jews in Romania, III: Between the Two World Wars* (Tel-Aviv: The Goldstein Goren Diaspora Research Center, 2005).

5 Dumitru, *The State, Antisemitism, and Collaboration*, 70–92.

Bessarabia and Northern Bukovina in summer 1940 in accordance with the Molotov-Ribbentrop Pact.[6] The so-called Russian Year that lasted from summer 1940 to summer 1941 led to a major transformation of society. For one, thousands of Romanians fled these areas, and the Romanian army was forced to retreat in great haste. For another, society was reorganized according to Soviet and Marxist-Leninist principles. Following years of incremental antisemitic discrimination in interwar Romania, a section of the Jewish population welcomed these changes, hopeful of what the Soviet model could offer. But as Margalith's own experience indicates, Jews were not spared from the harsh consequences of the Soviet takeover, including shortages of basic goods, political indoctrination and even terror.[7]

Still, worse was to come. Across the border in Romania, in summer 1940 and following the far-reaching territorial losses, Ion Antonescu, an army general who Carol 11 had asked to form a government, had subsequently forced the king to abdicate and taken power in an alliance with the Iron Guard. This marked the birth of the National Legionary State — a fascist-inspired authoritarian regime (1940–1941) followed by a military dictatorship, which lasted from 1941 to 1944. In this context, antisemitism grew even more extreme, and, in November 1940, Romania aligned itself militarily with the Axis. Then, in June 1941, Romania joined Nazi Germany in its attack on the Soviet Union. In the following years, with half a million troops, the Romanians became the Germans' closest military ally on the Eastern Front.

Edineți, the town in northern Bessarabia where Margalith Esterhuizen then lived, was one of the first places to be occupied in early July 1941. For Romanians, the aim was the "liberation" and "reintegration" of the lost land. This included retaliation against alleged

---

6 Although Northern Bukovina was not mentioned in the Molotov-Ribbentrop agreement, it was invaded anyway.

7 Among the thousands of people who were deported to Siberia by the Soviets during this time, there was a disproportionate number of Jews.

Judeo-Bolsheviks who had supposedly caused its loss and "the cleansing of the terrain" — namely the expulsion and murder of unwanted individuals and groups from this area.[8] For the Germans, the "war of extermination" against the Soviet Union had just begun. The convergence of these murderous campaigns proved especially brutal.

The Holocaust in Romania

What we now think of as the Holocaust in Romania had its own chronology, geography and set of perpetrators. It is usually broken down into stages, because distinctive policies and practices affected Jews in different parts of the country to varying degrees and in diverse ways. The first stage involved the already mentioned systematic disenfranchisement and discrimination of Jews in the entire country. Romania was the first European country outside of Nazi Germany to technically introduce legislation akin to the Nuremberg Laws for most Jews in August 1940. As Ezra Mendelsohn explains, "Jews were prohibited from owning land in villages, forbidden to publish newspapers, ousted from the army and denied any role in public life. They were forbidden to deal in goods over which there were state monopolies, to marry gentiles, and to convert to Christianity."[9] Under the influence of Nazi Germany and fascist-inspired movements throughout Europe, Romanians had taken the stance that Jews were a race rather than a religious group and that their presence in the country was undesirable.

The second stage involved the onset of physical violence against Jews in summer 1940. That July, a pogrom broke out in the northern Romanian town of Dorohoi. In the following months, across the country, Jews were attacked, beaten and thrown out of moving trains.

---

8 Vladimir Solonari, *Purifying the Nation: Population Exchange and Ethnic Cleansing in Nazi-Allied Romania* (Washington: Woodrow Wilson Press, 2010).

9 Mendelsohn, *The Jews of East Central Europe*, 208.

This phase culminated in the Bucharest pogrom in January 1941, during which more than one hundred Jews were murdered.

The third phase began with the genocidal crimes committed by the Romanian army, police and civilians in collaboration with the Germans amid the onset of war in summer 1941. Most well-known is the pogrom in Iași, Romania's second-largest city, at the end of June 1941, which resulted in the deaths of an estimated fourteen thousand men, women and children.[10] However, around this time dozens of ancillary massacres and pogroms took place as German and Romanian troops and the front moved across towns and villages of the recently reacquired borderland areas of Bukovina and Bessarabia. Between twelve thousand and twenty thousand Jews are believed to have been shot there in July and August 1941. This stage culminated in the mass murder of the Jews of Odessa (between fifteen thousand and twenty thousand people) by Romanian forces and the mass deportations of Jews who remained living in Bukovina and Bessarabia. These deportations started in summer and lasted until the end of the year. Hardly planned and chaotically implemented, this measure involved the forced marching of thousands of famished and destitute deportees, including the young, old and sick, for hundreds of miles, and their concentration in open-air transit camps and ghettos that have been described as "death pens" by historians.[11] In these appalling conditions, many died before reaching their destination, and many documents suggest this was the intention.

---

10 On this and other pogroms, see Jean Ancel, *Prelude to Mass Murder: The Pogrom in Iași, Romania, June 29, 1941 and Thereafter*, trans. Fern Seckbach (Jerusalem: Yad Vashem, 2013).

11 Although further deportations — also from the Romanian "Old Kingdom" — did take place in the following months and years, the scale was not comparable. On the case of Bessarabia and for the use of the expression "death pens," see Paul Shapiro, "Cleansing the Terrain in Bessarabia: In Towns, Transit Camps and Ghettos, Deportations," *Holocaust: Studii și cercetări* 14 (2021): 117–124.

xxii A LIGHT IN THE CLOUDS

Although these crimes were largely inspired by German plans and committed alongside German actions, they primarily took place independently. This is why the locations of the Holocaust in Romania are so different from those typically associated with the Holocaust and why the conditions of the persecution in the territory under Romanian rule displayed such specific dynamics, characteristics and conjunctures. Jews of Bukovina and Bessarabia were not deported to German concentration and death camps but to a territory known as Transnistria, a strip of land of about forty thousand square kilometres between the Dniester and Bug rivers in what is now southwestern Ukraine. Reaching from the city of Odessa (now Odesa) in the south to parts of the Vinnitsa District (Vinnytsia Oblast) in the north, the territory was carved out following the Tiraspol Agreement of August 20, 1941, with which the Germans granted Romania permission to administer it.[12]

Aside from Odessa, the Transnistria Governate was primarily rural and, after 1941, a war-torn area. With the help of the governor, Gheorghe Alexianu, Antonescu planned to exploit it like a colony and use it as a "dumping ground" for Jews, pending their deportation beyond the Bug River.[13] Ordinance 1 in August 1941 and Ordinance

---

12 Details concerning the administration were outlined in the Tighina Agreement, which came into force on August 30. Transnistria was meant to constitute compensation for Romania's loss of northern Transylvania to Hungary in summer 1940. However, hoping to eventually regain the western province, the Romanians never fully annexed their new eastern territory. On this, see Vladimir Solonari, *A Satellite Empire: Romanian Rule in Southwestern Ukraine, 1941–1944* (Ithaca: Cornell University Press, 2019).

13 For this expression, see Dennis Deletant, "Ghetto Experience in Golta, Transnistria, 1942–1944," *Holocaust and Genocide Studies* 18, no. 1 (2004): 1–26, p. 3. On the Holocaust in Transnistria, see Jean Ancel, *Transnistria: The Romanian Mass Murder Campaigns 1941–1942*, vols. 1–3 (Tel-Aviv, Goldstein Goren Diaspora Research Center, 2003); Dalia Ofer, "Life in the Ghettos of Transnistria," *Yad Vashem Studies* 25 (1996): 229–274.

23 in November 1941 established that Jews were to be concentrated in ghettos under local leadership. By then, the local Soviet Jewish population had already been decimated by the Romanian-German invasion.[14] But between September 15, 1941, and January 15, 1942, an estimated 118,847 Jews, mostly from Bukovina and Bessarabia (57,000 and 56,000, respectively), survivors of the bloody pogroms and massacres of the previous weeks and months, were deported to the area. They were split across five zones — Moghilev (55,913), Iampol (35,276), Râbnița (24,570), Tiraspol (872) and Iaska (2,216)[15] — and forced to live in approximately 150 makeshift camps and ghettos. Often these were just abandoned and derelict buildings or farms in the vicinity of a town or a designated and usually run-down part of an urban settlement. Most had a more or less porous border guarded by Romanian gendarmerie and armed forces and, in some cases, Ukrainian armed personnel.

Although a handful of the camps and ghettos were much larger, the majority had fewer than 150 inhabitants.[16] There were also significant differences between the camps in terms of living conditions and survival rates. In the south of Transnistria and along the eastern border, where the German influence was greater, the risk of being shot or taken to the German zone of occupation beyond the Bug for labour never to return was much higher. However, mobility was restricted everywhere, contact with family and friends forbidden, and livelihoods had to be gained, if at all, through forced labour

---

14 Of the 300,000 believed to have lived in the region before the war, an estimated 80,000 managed to flee into the Soviet interior, and only 15,000 survived. Ofer, "Life in the Ghettos of Transnistria," 232.

15 Ioanid, *The Holocaust in Romania*, 174. In present-day Ukraine, Moghilev is now known as Mohyliv-Podilskyi, Iampol as Yampil, and Iaska as Yas'ky.

16 Deletant, "Ghetto Experience in Golta," 6.

with practically no remuneration.[17] All over, epidemics, famine, over-crowding, a lack of basic goods, sanitation and hygiene, and exposure to the elements as well as arbitrary acts of violence were integral parts of everyday life.

Margalith and her family, who were forced to leave their home in August 1941, were likely among the first to be deported. Her account of this trajectory and subsequent events is not entirely clear — her memory most probably blurred by the temporal distance and traumatic character of the experiences. However, she appears to have been part of a group which was marched somewhat aimlessly for several days or even weeks, sleeping out in the open, if allowed to rest at all.[18] They eventually arrived, like many deportees to Transnistria, in the Bessarabian border town of Atachi (present-day Otaci) and then crossed over to Moghilev-Podolsk — the Ukrainian town just opposite Atachi on the eastern banks of the Dniester River. They were then sent on to the Murafa ghetto, located some seventy kilometres farther east, in the northern and central part of Transnistria. In this small town, deportees were forced to move in with local Jews and crammed into very small and rudimentary spaces.

According to Sarah Rosen, who has studied conditions in this ghetto specifically, an estimated 3,500 deportees arrived in Murafa between autumn 1941 and January 1942 and joined the 800 local

---

17 Work was remunerated in local currency, which was the German *Reichskredit-kassenschein* (RKKS) mark used in Soviet territories occupied by the Germans. Initially, one RKKS was the equivalent of ten rubles, but the exchange rate used was completely disproportionate to its real market value and this money was worthless.

18 See entry on "Edineți" by Ovidiu Creangă and Diana Dumitru in The United States Holocaust Memorial Museum, *Encyclopedia of Camps and Ghettos, 1933–1945 vol. III: Camps and Ghettos under European Regimes Aligned with Nazi Germany,* ed. Joseph R. White (Bloomington: Indiana University Press, 2018), 676–678, p. 677.

Jews who were living there.[19] Most of the newcomers were from the Bukovina and Dorohoi districts; however, a few hundred were from Bessarabia. An official count from September 1943, almost two years later, indicates that "800 local Jews and 2605 deportees lived in Murafa: 2179 (74 percent) were from Bukovina and 426 (26 percent) deportees from Bessarabia."[20] This was 1,100 fewer people than were believed to have lived there in March 1943. Still, with several thousand residents, Murafa was one of the largest of the fifty-three ghettos in the region, and some degree of contact with the other large and nearby ghettos of Moghilev, Shargorod and Djurin was established.

Life in the Transnistrian camps was characterized by widespread death, loss and abuse. The conditions were certainly distinct to what happened in other parts of Europe, and, most importantly, they did not result in complete annihilation. But the situation should nevertheless be divided into different phases. The first phase, which lasted until the spring or summer of 1942, was characterized by shock and high death rates (between 30 per cent and 50 per cent in the first winter). For the relatively wealthy Jews of Bukovina and Bessarabia in particular, the poor living conditions and the lack of infrastructure were unfathomable. Having had to sell all their belongings and valuables, they had to learn to live with the cold, hunger and disease. Typhus epidemics spread in waves across the camps, and many children were orphaned.

However, with time, an absurd kind of normality set in, and residents developed strategies of survival. A new and complex kind of society came about. Indeed, the second phase was one of adjustment and saw the establishment of self-government: the residents created institutions (leaderships, welfare offices and, in some cases, even

19 Sarah Rosen, "Surviving in the Murafa Ghetto: A Case Study of One Ghetto in Transnistria," *Holocaust Studies* 16, no. 1–2 (2010): 157–176, pp. 161–162.
20 Rosen, "Surviving in the Murafa Ghetto," p. 162.

courts and a police force), set up small workshops and businesses and ran hospitals and doctors' practices.[21] Although these institutions had a limited capacity and there were tensions among the different groups, these structures made a major difference. Rosen, for instance, argues that the relatively high survival rate in the Murafa ghetto was due to the degree of such self-organization.[22] Many residents also traded with local Ukrainians. Leaving the ghettos on one's own account was often possible albeit dangerous: those caught outside the ghetto area were subject to beatings, imprisonment or even shot and killed. However, bribery was widespread, and skills such as speaking Ukrainian could prove essential. Family and community networks were also very important. Ana Bărbulescu has spoken of the development of a "network of trust" alongside a "network of aggressiveness" and highlighted the strategies people developed to avoid perilous situations: "the official order enforced by the authorities was paralleled by a set of social practices developed by the ghettos' inmates, that allowed them to circumvent the collective definition imposed by the broader society and by the Romanian authorities."[23] In this context, as the case of Margalith Esterhuizen shows, children and young people, who could pass more easily as locals or elicit compassion from villagers, had a specific kind of agency.[24]

With time, therefore, hope that it might be possible to survive this ordeal tended to grow. Crucially, Romanian policy toward Jews changed considerably as the German military situation deteriorated.

---

21 Gali Tibon, "Am I My Brother's Keeper? The Jewish Committees in the Ghettos of Mogilev Province and the Romanian Regime in Transnistria during the Holocaust, 1941–1944," *Dapim: Studies on the Holocaust* 30, no. 2 (2016): 93–116.

22 Rosen, "Surviving in the Murafa Ghetto," 158, 165.

23 Ana Bărbulescu, "Parallel Worlds of the Holocaust in Romania: Legitimizing, Witnessing, and Avoiding Death," *Holocaust: Studii și cercetări 7* (2015): 195–204, p. 202.

24 On this, see Ofer, "Life in the Ghettos of Transnistria," 256–259.

At the end of 1942, Antonescu put an end to widespread killings. The situation of deportees also improved, especially from 1943 onward, thanks to the delivery of aid (food, clothing, medicine and money) sent by the Aid Committee in Bucharest. At the end of 1943, the Antonescu regime approved the repatriation of selected groups, such as orphans, to take them to Palestine.[25] In the following months, some 10,744 Jews, including some 1,960 orphans, were repatriated from Transnistria.[26] Although she technically was not orphaned and was almost too old to qualify, Margalith was registered and returned to Romania, first to Chişinău (Kishinev) and later to Iaşi in early 1944. The Murafa ghetto was liberated by the Red Army and dissolved a few months later, on March 19, 1944.

Margalith remained in foster care until she was able to board a train for Turkey and then a ship for Palestine in May 1945. The events of the war and the Holocaust, therefore, tore her family apart: living on different continents but also on different sides of the Cold War divide, she could not see her parents until the 1960s in Kiev, in the Soviet Union (now Kyiv, Ukraine). Still, she was one of the lucky ones. An

---

25 This move was something the Jewish leaders had long been lobbying for, and it was the result of ongoing negotiations between Jewish organizations, international bodies such as the International Committee of the Red Cross and the War Refugee Board, and the Romanian government. The repatriations themselves were organized and financed by a range of different Zionist agencies and Jewish organizations. On this, see Wilhelm Filderman, *Memoirs & Diaries, vol. 2, 1940–1952* (Jerusalem: Yad Vashem, 2015). Radu Ioanid, "The Destruction and Rescue of Jewish Children in Bessarabia, Bukovina, and Transnistria (1941–1944)," in *Children and the Holocaust: Symposium Presentation* (Washington: Center for Holocaust Studies United States Holocaust Memorial Museum, 2004); Dana Mihăilescu, "Networks of Sutured Consciousness in Early Holocaust Testimonies of Orphaned Jewish Child Survivors from Romania," in *Starting Anew: The Rehabilitation of Child Survivors of the Holocaust in the Early Postwar Years*, eds. Sharon Kansiger Kohen and Dalia Ofer (Jerusalem: Yad Vashem, 2019).

26 Ioanid, "The Destruction and Rescue of Jewish Children," 88.

estimated 280,000 men, women and children were killed or let die in Transnistria, and only around 70,000 survived; just 12,000 of those survivors were from Bessarabia. Most of Margalith's relatives, including her grandparents on both sides, were killed in the Holocaust.

Postwar

Margalith Esterhuizen's postwar experiences and trajectory might be regarded as both unique and emblematic. Most Romanian Jews emigrated from Romania to Palestine and later Israel in the first years after the war, and, among those who left, survivors from Bessarabia, Bukovina and Transnistria were overrepresented. As others have noted, postwar Romania was barely recognizable, and the Holocaust largely marked the start of the protracted end of Romanian Jewish life and history. However, as Margalith herself points out, the energy with which she embraced a new land and language and rapidly rebuilt her life was the exception, not the rule. She describes herself as eager to learn and learning as a source of self-assurance and healing. In Israel, she found new values, belonging and a sense of purpose. In the following decades, making a home for herself and her family, first in South Africa and later in Canada, she continued to prove over and over her ability to adapt, remain curious and reinvent herself. Her account is therefore not just the testimony of a Holocaust survivor. It is also a testament to one person's exceptional resilience and strength, and an exploration of the immigrant experience in some of the most extreme circumstances. Writing this memoir was undoubtedly, as Margalith Esterhuizen writes in the preface, an "agonizing" task. However, we are hugely grateful she chose to do so.

Gaëlle Fisher
Leibniz Institute for Contemporary History
Munich-Berlin, 2022

ROMANIA DURING WORLD WAR II

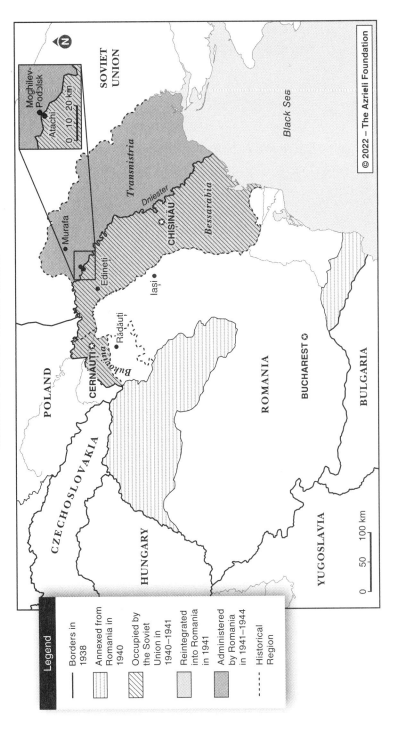

Legend

Borders in
1938

Annexed from
Romania in
1940

Occupied by
the Soviet
Union in
1940–1941

Reintegrated
into Romania
in 1941

Administered
by Romania
in 1941–1944

Historical
Region

SOVIET
UNION

Moghilev-
Podolsk
Atachi
0 10 20 km

Transnistria

Dniester

Murafa

Edineți

CHIȘINĂU

Bessarabia

Iași

Rădăuți

CERNĂUȚI

Bukovina

POLAND

CZECHOSLOVAKIA

HUNGARY

ROMANIA

BUCHAREST

BULGARIA

YUGOSLAVIA

Black Sea

0   50   100 km

© 2022 – The Azrieli Foundation

I dedicate this story of my life to the memory of my beloved husband, my three amazing sons and my five beautiful grandchildren. Thank you for your support, endless love and understanding, without which it would not have been possible.

Author's Preface

It is difficult to explain how agonizing a task it has been trying to recall my wartime experiences. I spent years in South Africa trying to forget my past by living as normal a life as possible, as a young wife and mother raising children, working and trying to assimilate into a new country that had its own political and racial problems.

For years, I was haunted by nightmares, and my husband would shake me awake saying that I was screaming in a peculiar, unnatural, strangled voice. There were many times when I tried to recall those dark memories, but it became too painful. The memories would cause me to shake in pure anguish, which caused me to postpone writing my memoir. Now, age has caught up with me, and I've come to realize that my story must be told to be added to all the other survivor stories. It took many years and a lot of painful soul-searching to enable me to write about the horrors of my wartime experiences, the Holocaust years. But this is the story of my life, and the world needs to know it.

I am well aware that at some point in my past I should have told my sons and family what it meant to be a Jew in Europe in the 1930s and how I survived the Holocaust. Until now they have not been told my entire personal story partly because I found it difficult to open up and tell them about the senseless cruelty, horror and suffering I and many others endured. I was also aware that my experiences would be a burden in my sons' young lives, causing them sadness, hatred and even prejudice toward those responsible for this outrage. I was determined for them to grow up free of my past, to live without pain and fears.

I know I accomplished some of my goal.

Today, I contemplate my wonderful, amazing and loving family, of which I am so proud, and my beloved husband and partner, who is no longer with us. I know the time to tell my story to the best of my ability is now, before it is simply too late.

The Romania of My Past

It all started in Romania, the country of my birth.

About that short period of my life before the war I have images, memories, of a nurturing, loving home among a large, gregarious, close family of grandparents, uncles, aunts and many cousins. The Holocaust destroyed our family in Romania, tore it apart; with the exception of one aunt, I never heard of or saw any of my extended family again.

The Romania I knew in my childhood was a land of song and dances. The *doina*, Romanian folk music, is made up of stirring songs and laments. It was a land where colourful hand-embroidered national costumes, with colourful ribbons for a headdress were worn with pride, mostly on national holidays and celebratory occasions.

Farmers raised sheep and cattle, tilled and worked their fertile lands under blue skies. Schools taught French as a second language. We all loved to eat *mămăligă*, the national cornmeal dish, with milk or gravy; when set, *mămăligă* could be sliced like a cake. *Cozonac* was a large plain cake prepared with eggs, sugar and flour baked mostly at Easter. Boiled eggs painted in a variety of many dazzling colours would also make their appearance at Easter.

Romania was a modern European country. Its capital, Bucharest, was cosmopolitan, lively, teeming with tourists. In fact, Bucharest was often dubbed "little Paris." Romania also has popular sandy beaches along the Black Sea, such as Mamaia, a coastal beach front I remember as a particularly beautiful resort. Romania's Carpathian Mountains are also well known, surrounded by verdant valleys, pastures and hills, in a moderate climate conducive to growing fine fruit, vegetables, flowers and more.

~

My beloved sister, Dorica, was born on August 4, 1925, and I made my appearance nearly two years later, on July 28, 1927. I wish I had more details of our lost childhood years. I had the opportunity, when my father was alive, to ask him about those early years of my life, and sadly I did not. I have pieced together details of my parents' lives, their marriage, to the best of my ability using snippets related to me by family members over the years. There are no documents available about them and their backgrounds, since during the war years all our personal documents, such as birth certificates, were seized and destroyed, and we became displaced. To make matters worse, there are no living family members to help me in this respect.

My parents' marriage was arranged according to traditional Jewish custom called *shidduch,* a Yiddish term meaning a match or matchmaking. In this custom, young women are discouraged from freely dating or choosing their partners, and their parents choose the likely groom. Parents make the decision for their sons or daughters based on family background (finances played a large part), and the would-be groom's future prospects were obviously of great importance. The match was deemed to be satisfactory only if both sets of parents on each side agreed. The couple's fate was agreed upon first, and only then a meeting between the two young people would take place, arranged and duly supervised, or chaperoned, by their elders, of course. What happened if the would-be bride was not attracted to her chosen groom? Oy — who knows?

My parents, Rachel Maimon and Moritz Srul Herscovici, married in 1923 and started their life together in the small town of Rădăuți, perhaps to be close to my mother's parents, the Maimons, who also lived there. Rădăuți, which at that time was part of the region of southern Bukovina, was in northern Romania, not too far from the Soviet Ukraine border. The area was known for farming, and my grandfather owned and ran a grain produce business. My maternal grandparents were solid, God-fearing, decent and hard-working people.

My sister and I used to look forward to our visits with our grandparents, whom we loved. After we had moved away to the city, visiting them on our vacations offered a change from city life and was a magical, unforgettable experience. We would run through their large open land carefree and happy, marvelling at all sorts of exciting treasures never encountered in the city: birds, insects, pretty, slow-flying butterflies, wildflowers, stones, trees. Everything was new and a source of joy to us.

I recall the huge farm-style warehouse on their land and their large, spacious home, which once accommodated their seven children. I can almost still smell and taste the wonderful fragrance of our grandma's cooking and endless baking of delicious Jewish delights. I don't recall ever being there when she was not in the kitchen. Dear kind Boba — what we called our grandma — always had time for endearing words and a warm cuddle for both of us. Boba was short, rotund and had a wonderful disposition. A copious apron wrapped around her body at all times. She delighted in cooking those well-known, unforgettable traditional Jewish meals and treats using recipes handed down through many generations. She baked the most wonderful cakes, desserts and cookies for us, causing tantalizing aromas to waft through the house.

Grandfather worked tirelessly on the land from dawn till late afternoon. We were not awake when he left at the crack of dawn; at the end of the day, he would return from the fields tired, thoughtful and always quiet. Boba would greet him and hand him a cup of black tea with a slice of lemon. We would watch, fascinated, as he drank his tea from the saucer, either out of habit or perhaps to cool it down. He would then wait for his dinner silently, deep in thought, his fingers drumming endlessly on the surface of their mahogany hutch that displayed dainty china cups, plates and other collectibles. Its highly polished surface — in particular a section of it — bore witness to his constant tapping, causing the wood to show through, a result of his tapping absentmindedly for goodness knows how long, and always on the same place. Needless to say, tapping on the hutch — or anywhere else for that matter — was totally forbidden to my sister and me. It's funny what details stay in my mind all this time, never fading.

Now, as I recall all these memories, I close my eyes and visualize that happy period of my childhood. I am again with my grandparents, surrounded by their endless, loving care, one of the most cherished experiences of my extremely short childhood.

On my father's side were our Herscovici grandparents who lived in the small town of Herța (now Hertsa, Ukraine), which had a small Jewish population at the time. They had three children — my father, my aunt Gisele and another daughter, who died before I was born, of unknown causes, at the age of twenty-one. I've been told I am named after her. When my sister and I were growing up, we didn't know our paternal grandparents as well as we did our maternal grandparents.

Grandfather, extremely Orthodox, or *frum*, had the distinction of being one notch below a rabbi — qualified to perform religious rites and duties both in the synagogue and from home. He was a distinguished looking man who always wore a wide-brimmed hat and dark long frock coat, the kind worn by the devout. He grew twirling sidelocks, called *peyes*, and a large beard. He was a good, honest man, well liked and respected, always available for anyone who needed him, even though he also had a sombre demeanour and rarely smiled.

Grandmother was just as devout. Her clothes always covered her entire body, arms and legs, and a brown wig covered her head, tied away from her face in a chignon. I never found out if she had her own hair, but I always wondered. Strict Orthodox rules forbade Jewish women to show their hair, so her head was always covered by a scarf and tied under her chin.

During the Holocaust, all of my beloved grandparents were innocent victims of unimaginable cruelty. My paternal grandparents would suffer the same fate as my maternal grandparents — driven from their home mercilessly in the first months of the German occupation of Romania. My paternal grandfather most likely died on a death march from Herța, and my grandmother died after surviving for some time with my aunt Gisele in the ghettos of Transnistria. My maternal grandparents perished alone, with no family by their side. They must have been frightened and bewildered, and I have always thought they were among the first of many Jews to die.

Near Escapes and Upheavals

In 1930, antisemitism was slowly but surely beginning to rear its ugly head in Romania. My parents saw what was happening, and their fear of the implications for our future ultimately convinced them to make the difficult decision to leave Romania — to escape whatever was coming. They wanted to build a new life for our little family in what was then called Palestine — Eretz Yisrael, the Land of Israel. After careful consideration, Father resigned from his job as an accountant at a local sugar refining factory.

Amid feverish packing and preparations, and endless, tearful goodbyes to family and friends, our belongings were loaded onto a ship and we soon proceeded to make our way to Palestine with high hopes and enthusiasm, eagerly looking forward to a new and better life. Palestine was thought of as the ultimate haven, with certain Jewish prayers since time immemorial including the words "Next year in Jerusalem" — Jews forever dreaming of life in a country of our own, free of persecution.

I was much too young in 1930 to recall the voyage to Palestine, but these events were related to me through the years, allowing me to retain some of those details. What happened after the voyage decided our entire future. We arrived in the Port of Haifa, excited, starry-eyed and eager to disembark in the land of our hopes, ready to start our new life. However, destiny — in the form of British officialdom, since Palestine was then under a British mandate — intervened. Our

documents were pored over, examined in minute detail, and declared
to be totally inadequate. My parents' pleas, insistence and appeals
were ignored. No other avenue seemed open to us; there was no
embassy to contact. We were not permitted to disembark the ship
and were forced to remain on board waiting for the ship to return
to Romania. I have always thought that we may have been blocked
not because of our papers but by a new anti-Jewish preference being
enforced by the British officials.

Regardless, my father would have had no way of researching all
the necessary information about immigration. All we knew was that
other people had successfully immigrated to British Mandate Palestine before us. Unfortunately, we found ourselves in the unenviable
and completely unexpected situation of having failed to reach our
anticipated freedom.

Perhaps to lessen their own disappointment and frustration, my
parents decided to make a family holiday of our return trip, and so we
toured Turkey and Greece before heading back to Romania. We visited many well-known, magnificent sites in both countries in the few
weeks before returning to Romania, though I remember very little of
our unexpected adventure.

Despite our recent setbacks, our parents were determined to do
the best they could under the circumstances to start a new life back in
Romania. Having resigned his position at the sugar refining factory,
Father had to find new ways of making a living. Instead of returning
to Rădăuți, my parents decided to settle in Cernăuți in the region of
northern Bukovina (now Chernivtsi, Ukraine).

Cernăuți in 1931 was a beautiful, established city with large, gran-
diose and picturesque buildings and homes. Deep in my subcon-
scious, I remember visiting a distant, newly discovered relative in the
city living in a large, character home of untold beauty. It had huge
halls, beautifully adorned, and was elegantly furnished. Cernăuți was
lively, ultra-modern, cultured and fashionable, its wide streets illumi-
nated at night by tall old street lights. It had earned for itself the title

of "another little Paris," and a great many wanted to live in and be part of this city that was so rich in culture, with music venues, opera, theatres and museums.

We rented a two-bedroom apartment in a well-kept building centrally situated close to schools and many amenities. My sister started school and I was enrolled in kindergarten. Our home was cheerful and happy. We began to make friends, and life was good.

My father found a position with a new and exciting German company called Blaupunkt that marketed and sold radios, which were still a novelty product back then. These radios were well made — sturdy, large and heavy. It was a new experience for us to hear marvellous sounds coming out of a box, something we had never heard or seen before. Father travelled extensively by train to promote the radio, covering a large part of Bukovina. Marketing the new product took him away from us and we missed him a lot.

Mother did not work outside the home. By nature lively and sociable, she made friends easily. Mother had a lot of time on her hands, and she developed a passion for the game of poker, playing as often as she could with her group of friends either at our home or elsewhere, mostly when Father was away. The games were played for high stakes, higher than we could afford, and Mother often lost her housekeeping allowance, which caused serious consequences. However, Mother was a talented crafter, excellent at crochet work, and used her skills to produce magnificent tablecloths, bed covers, curtains and other exquisite pieces for which she became well known. She often sold her work to cover her considerable losses.

Her gambling and Father's frequent trips away from home eventually took their toll on my parents' marriage. Their relationship began to deteriorate, and Father stayed away more often than he had to, or so it felt. They did not argue in our presence, but we still knew our mother was unhappy and seeking distractions.

In those days, divorce was not really an option. They remained together despite their unhappiness — perhaps for our sakes, hard to know. Yet, we did not suffer in any way. During the summers, my sister and I were either enrolled in day camps or taken on a train voyage to stay with our maternal grandparents.

Then, in either 1935 or 1936, Mother accidentally cut into one of her fingers while cleaning cooking pots with a wad of coarse steel wool. It was a deep cut that bled non-stop. Eventually the bleeding was contained and she bandaged her finger, but a few days later it was swollen and painful. The wound was obviously infected; in fact, the infection spread partly to her arm. A doctor she visited hospitalized her immediately due to her high fever. At first, she was treated for pneumonia, but the infection spread, causing a severe blood infection and eventual gangrene. Naturally I had absolutely no knowledge of the medical profession of the time, and it probably was not as advanced or specialized as it has become. Doctors tried to halt the infection but by that time it had spread mercilessly. Her arm needed to be amputated to save her life, but she refused. Doctors tried everything else they could to save Mother's life but failed; she was only thirty-five when the toxins in her blood killed her.

The loss of my mother is difficult and painful to describe. It was traumatic — we did not understand what had happened; when we did, we could not come to terms with the reality. My sister, Dorica, was ten and I was eight. Our world completely fell apart.

Bewildered and in great pain, we could not contemplate a future without our loving and much beloved mother. Later, as I got older, I realized that Mother must have been unhappy, and she might have chosen to die rather than have her arm amputated because she had lost her will to live.

A period of shiva followed, where daily prayers were said, giving us time to mourn. But soon after her death, my mother's three sisters arrived. Without us understanding what was happening, her sisters packed all our mother's magnificent hand crocheted pieces plus all her personal items and then left, taking everything with them. Strangely, nothing was left for us to remember her by.

Father, grieving Mother's death and unable to cope with bringing up his two children on his own, arranged for us to live with his parents until he could put his life back together. We were about to embark on dramatic changes for which we were unprepared and ill-equipped. We had no choice but to do what we were told, and that was to live with our paternal grandparents until Father could establish a home for us again.

Our grandparents agreed to care for us, but we had spent little time with them in the past. In their care, we faced a completely new order. We had to learn how to live with our ultra-Orthodox grandparents and play by their rules, which were strict and had to be followed to the letter. Our days included frequent visits to their synagogue and a new school but also, with some luck, new friends.

It could not have been easy for our grandparents either, faced with the prospect of looking after two very hurt and bewildered girls. But we were family and they loved us. They were willing to give us a temporary home no matter what.

We learned a lot in that period that we did not know before. Friday was the day food was prepared for the Sabbath, which started at sunset. During the Sabbath there was no work of any kind, and in their household, neither play nor even visiting was allowed — only walks to the synagogue at least twice during the day, and rest. My grandparents hired a non-Jewish person for that day to light the stove to warm our food, as well as to do any manual work while we prayed, ate our meals and rested during the day, until sunset on Saturday.

Our father visited us at regular intervals or whenever he was able to. The separation was as tough on him as it was on us, and we knew we had to wait until he could make a home for us. The waiting was difficult, and we tried our best to be patient.

It was on one of these visits, after eight or nine months had passed since our mother's death, that he told us about a woman he had met whom he liked very much. Ethel was eighteen years younger than him and single. He told us he wanted to marry her. He wanted to know how we felt about it. It meant we would have a home again, be a family and have a stepmother. He assured us that Ethel was kind and would welcome us with open arms. We wanted him to be happy and also wanted to be part of his life again. We wanted our life to be as it was before.

Father and Ethel married almost exactly one year after Mother's death, as was the custom, given the traditional mourning period. They settled in the town of Lipcani at first. My sister and I were looking forward to being with Father and wanted our life to return to normal, but that was not yet possible. Secretly neither of us looked forward to having a stepmother. It wasn't until many years later, when it was much too late, that I realized Ethel was a rare and wonderful person who treated us very well. The two of us by no means made life easy for her, nor did we try to get to know her. Only now do I realize what a huge undertaking it must have been for her, raising two ungrateful girls, caring for us and providing us with a fine home, which we took for granted.

A year or so later, Father and Ethel gave up their home in Lipcani, deciding instead to move to Edineți, a town where Ethel's large family had lived for many years. Enrolled in school in Edineți, my sister and I began to make new friends. It was a school run by Catholic nuns of a German order. Those nuns were excellent teachers, dedicated and kind. One of the subjects taught was home crafts. It is from these German nuns that I learned the craft of knitting — which I still enjoy to this day — in what seemed to be a totally different, simpler and faster style than is common now.

Before long, our lives took on a sense of normalcy, and it was a life that both of us enjoyed and adapted to with ease. Our stepmother's family took an interest in us and soon became our extended family. Father was relaxed, happy and content. Ethel was without a doubt a culinary wizard who, with what seemed to be little effort, produced delicious meals, cakes and pastries worthy of kings. She kept house and was always doing something. She constantly tried to win over us two very ungrateful, selfish girls.

The kitchen was her domain where she ruled like a queen. Sometimes she would involve us in mixing her cake batter, which in those times was an art in itself, with none of the electric mixing gadgets available today. At first she tested us, and when she was satisfied that we could do a decent job, she would allow us to help her. We were put to work mixing batter with a large wooden spoon. Not an easy task, tiring, and so we took turns mixing, making sure the end result was acceptable because it had to be of a certain consistency to meet her high standards. The reward for us would come once the mixture was ready — after she used the batter, we were allowed to take turns licking the bowl and wooden spoon. Inevitably, this ended in a very ugly brawl between the two of us, resulting in the batter somehow finding its way on our respective heads and hair — not a pretty sight! Ethel took our squabbles calmly, never chastising or punishing us, and she did not let on she was unhappy with us; she never lifted her hand to us, although she must have been sorely tempted many times.

It was to be the start of a new life for the four of us, a time to get to know each other better, a time of healing and settling down.

When Childhood Ended

The summer of 1940 was a bleak time in Romania. World War II had started the year before, and now the Romanian monarchy was in trouble. The Soviet Union, Hungary and Bulgaria were all in dispute with Romania over its borders, planning to take over parts of its territory.

It did not take long before these border disputes resulted in a loss of land. At the end of June and beginning of July, the Soviets occupied parts of Romania and its army invaded our region; soldiers marched in rhythm, singing and carrying their red flags triumphantly, as if they were conquerors.

From somewhere, loudspeakers broadcasted propaganda slogans and speeches. The "Internationale," the unofficial anthem of the Soviet Union, boomed loudly and could be heard for miles. Amid much excitement and merriment, soldiers were greeted by the majority of the population with great joy, flowers and the waving of small red flags, hailing the new governing forces and voicing approval. Next, large red flags bearing the hammer and sickle fluttered from many buildings, and some had Stalin's image on them for good measure.

Farmers envisaging a better life under Communism were elated at the prospect of participating in communal farming, foreseeing all the benefits they would reap as farmers under a new regime. They were dreaming.

For days afterward, soldiers were everywhere. The streets were full of soldiers mingling with the population and basking in their obvious popularity.

But in only a few days after the occupation, life as we knew it changed completely. Essential, ordinary consumer goods like bread, milk, eggs, sugar, butter and flour began to disappear from grocery shelves, leaving most stores empty. Food of any sort became scarce and was at an absolute premium. Long lines formed daily outside bakeries for the purchase of a single loaf of bread, now rationed.

In their total disregard for the fundamental needs of the people, the Soviets commandeered all food items in our town, stripping us of all supplies. These items were taken to feed their soldiers, with no regard or care for the people who had so vigorously and wholeheartedly hailed their arrival. What a letdown for everyone, especially for all those hard-working farmers who were hoping for a better life under Communism.

An anecdote was doing the rounds at that time. The sudden shortage of consumer goods prompted someone to ask a soldier what, if anything, the Soviet Union manufactured. "Everything," came the quick response. "What about lemons?" "Oh, sure, we have factories making those as well."

We began to get used to food shortages, avidly following notifications when a new supply of certain items was expected. Although it meant lining up for hours on end, no one asked questions; everyone complied.

School resumed that fall without undue delay. My sister and I were still in the school run by Catholic nuns, but the Romanian curriculum was no longer being taught. I was thirteen, and my sister was fifteen. The soft-spoken nuns explained that there were new laws now in effect. The Communist regime evidently did not tolerate religion, which made the kind Catholic nuns extremely nervous.

We were at school to learn, and learn we did. A Russian teacher was promptly found and the process of learning the Russian language began. Learning Russian was now mandatory, and indoctrination followed immediately. Where better than schools? We were forced to wear the three-cornered Soviet red scarf in class as part of our school uniform. Daily gymnastics, flag-waving and huge, fluttering red flags bearing the hammer and sickle emblem appeared at school, as did crude, hastily made banners bearing slogans, such as "Proletarians of the world, unite!"

One good thing about the Soviets was that they believed in physical culture: a healthy mind in a healthy body. Every child was expected to participate in daily exercises, which Dorica and I began to enjoy.

We continued to learn to cope with the new regime, doing our best to deal with the new regulations and hoping that in time we would get used to the Soviet occupation. We continued to be well taken care of at home by our stepmother and even made a few new friends. We always had Ethel's baking to look forward to. Plus, she still kept us busy mixing her cake batter and other small chores.

But in that fall of 1940, the dormant, underlying hatred of Jews — which no doubt had existed for countless years in the country — was exploding in Romania. A movement called the Iron Guard was expanding, whose members wore green uniforms and devoted their time to terrorizing helpless Jews. There was nothing now to hold them back; they were in their element, having the backing of the Romanian government. A period of lawlessness had begun; the police seemed to vanish or may very well have been part of the new movement. All we saw were these green-shirted individuals spreading terror everywhere they could.

Then, almost one year after the Soviet occupation, unbelievably and without any warning or loss of life, the scene abruptly changed. Overnight, the dreaded German and Romanian armies arrived, marching in ceremoniously. It was a show of threatening might when troops wearing high boots marched in. It is difficult to forget the sound of the German army — their rhythmic, clicking steps in

unison as they marched, their endless tanks, a variety of heavy arma-
ments parading through the main street for all to see. The intention
was probably to intimidate the population. To me, it felt as though
Germany was taking over the country, a part of their quest to control
and occupy all of Eastern Europe. The Nazis and the other Axis pow-
ers, which included Romania, had pushed the Soviets out of Edineți
and were invading the Soviet Union and Soviet-occupied areas.

The population did not welcome the German and Romanian
armies. People stayed home, listening intently and nervously to news
on radios in fear and horror of what was to come. My sister and I
were not told much but we sensed awful changes that were taking
place almost overnight. It was as if a huge dark cloak had descended,
enveloping us in a sense of deep, grim foreboding. We heard adults
whispering, and their conversation stopped when we entered a room,
as parents do to protect their children's innocence. We were young,
but old enough to understand the implications of what was happening around us.

It was to be the end, the loss of everything we knew — home, sta-
bility, comfort, school and our peaceful existence, the normal family
life we had started to get used to. Although we were still totally un-
aware of how tragically the situation would affect each one of us, for
my sister and me, and countless others, the arrival of the Germans
and Romanians heralded the brutal end of our childhood.

～

Even with these scary events swirling around our lives, we enjoyed
the start of a beautiful, warm summer and were anticipating the many
autumn activities we loved. Both my sister and I were avid readers of
children's books of that time: Aesop's fables, Hans Christian Andersen
and the Brothers Grimm's tales. We allowed our imaginations to take
us on flights of fancy, helping us escape fleetingly, while in reality
waiting for the worst.

Every Jewish person knew to expect trouble. Rumours were circulating, and although my father tried to shield us, we were aware that something dark and menacing was taking place. It had started earlier that year when the Iron Guard members erupted in violence, breaking any and all shop windows owned by Jews, terrorizing owners, looting, doing everything they could to instill fear. They had beaten and kicked anyone who protested or stood up against them. Lawlessness had prevailed. It was hard for us to comprehend the situation. Even though the Iron Guard had been dismantled by the Romanian government, their antisemitic ideology had permeated through so much of society that to many it felt like they were still everywhere, now working closely and in total unison with the Germans. Their relations with the Germans sealed their hatred of Jews and intensified it through all the propaganda against us.

Antisemitism, which had already been at a boiling point, now surfaced openly. It was soon obvious that the Germans had complete and total cooperation from the Romanian leader at the time, Ion Antonescu, who willingly aided and abetted them in every way he could. He proved to a powerful and staunch ally.

Under the German and Nazi-aligned Romanian regime, antisemitism erupted and spilled over like lava from a volcano. Stories began to circulate regarding serious antisemitic incidents, stories of indescribable, senseless cruelty like beatings, looting, humiliation, ridicule and torment. I did not hear of the mass murders that were happening near us at this time. A cloak of fear and despair enveloped the terrorized local Jewish population.

Orders were posted in central places announcing that every Jewish person was to wear a Star of David, an armband or a visible patch anywhere on their person when venturing in the streets. Everyone followed the orders to wear the star, overwhelmed by feelings of disbelief, stark fear and deep humiliation; there was no choice, no one to whom we could appeal, no one who could or would listen. Other laws came into effect that forced shopkeepers and factory owners to abandon their businesses. Some schools closed.

We found ourselves in a singularly horrific situation beyond understanding. Gone was the peaceful, orderly life we had enjoyed surrounded by Ethel's extended family. All at once our non-Jewish friends we'd regularly spend time with began to distance themselves from us, forbidden by their parents to mix with us. Every non-Jewish person did all they could to avoid contact with us even if we accidentally met in the street. Complete indoctrination was born of the fear of the inevitable repercussions of not complying.

It's hard to explain how we continued to live each day in helpless fear and trepidation. Simply surviving through this agonizing time became vital: self-preservation was our goal. Deep inside our souls we dreamed of an uprising against the Nazis, anything to make it go away. We lived in hope that the situation we were experiencing would not continue. Salvation had to come in some form — the world must have known our plight and would save us. But we hoped in vain.

My sister and I, in our innocence, took refuge in our books and grew closer, spending as much time as possible together and finding ways of making the best of our forced inactivity indoors.

This insane situation continued while we held our breath, trying to be courageous. We lived like underground moles, mostly unseen, expecting some changes for the better and hoping that the rest of the population would band together in an uprising and oust the German occupation. It did not happen. Obviously, no one cared about their Jewish neighbours.

And so surviving each day continued to be our goal; it took every ounce of bravery we possessed just to get through a single day. Life to each Jewish person was even more precious, determined as we were to stay strong and keep hoping for salvation and survival.

The Endless March

Dark, menacing clouds gathered in the sky that fateful day in August 1941. It was as if even the heavens were sad and angry on the day the officials in Edineţi received orders for our evacuation.

On every street corner, loudspeakers loudly proclaimed the dreaded news: persons of Jewish faith were being evacuated. The words sent cold shivers through each and every one of us. We sensed that this would be the cruel end for all of us.

We were directed to assemble in the local town centre on a given day and to listen for further orders. We were to abandon our homes immediately, taking only strictly necessary personal items, which we would carry. We would be leaving behind our homes and everything our parents worked for all their lives to be left to a faceless multitude of Jew haters. We were told we would be evacuated without further delay, but no destination was given. There would be no reprieve for anyone, not even for those who were disabled, sick, babies, pregnant or aged. No one was exempt.

Anyone who remained in their homes would be shot. Some folks who stayed in their homes, people who were unable to walk, were indeed murdered on the spot. No mercy was shown to anyone.

There was no alternative and certainly no escaping. We could not flee because there was nowhere we could go, nowhere we could hide.

My father had the unenviable and heartbreaking task of explaining to us exactly what was taking place. In a tremulous, endearing voice filled with his special brand of kindness (it still haunts me to this day), he began explaining the unexplainable in his own words, describing the situation being forced upon us.

How does anyone tell their young children that their lives as they knew them are gone forever, that evil and hatred of our race has triumphed? That in their madness, the Nazis and their Romanian collaborators wanted to "purify" their race and in the process annihilate us?

The situation was beyond understanding and almost impossible to accept. To survive, there was no other option but to follow orders and what might come. Father told us to be brave, to do as we were told and to above all stay together to face our unknown future as best as we could. He made us understand we were forced to leave our home and lives behind.

It took us hours to decide what we needed to take. We would be walking to an unknown destination. We each needed to find warm clothes and to then carefully choose what we treasured most, bundling up only what we could wear or carry. Anything left behind would be looted. Ancient synagogues and Torahs were left to the mercy of ruthless individuals bent on destroying everything we valued and which gave meaning to our lives.

All at once, everything we owned had become precious and important, and it was difficult to decide what we could take with us. Dorica and I were so young, bewildered and confused. This was no preparation for a joyful holiday at the sea but a painful march into the unknown, a desperate situation with no foreseeable end in sight. We had in our possession the warm clothing and boots, which we wore, a blanket and a pillow; my father and stepmother, in addition to their own necessities, carried food supplies and some valuables ingeniously hidden somewhere on our stepmother's ample body. I also had a treasured gold locket. It had my late mother's image on the inside, and I wore it around my neck. It gave me a sense of comfort, even protection. It was later taken from me by soldiers who ordered all of us, under threat, to surrender valuables willingly or risk having them taken from us by force.

I can still vividly recall all these years later the hopelessness of that day when the loudspeakers bellowed out the final orders to leave. A cold day, wet and dark, the sky covered by swollen grey clouds enveloping us in sadness and utter despair. As I mentioned, it was almost as if even the heavens were mourning that fateful day in sympathy with our fearsome, horrific plight.

When we were told to assemble in the local square, we were all herded together, each of us carrying our bundle. I still remember seeing our people coming from all directions, a sad, pitiful, infinitely miserable procession of humanity.

Groups of families made their way to the square all bundled up against the weather. People just kept coming, the old, the frail, the infirm, many supported by family members, babies in arms, small children, pregnant women; it was a heart-wrenching, unforgettable sight. Long columns of people started to form that stretched out of the square.

Many appeared paralyzed by fear. The air filled with heartbreaking sounds of humanity's misery. We heard the sounds of praying, chanting loudly, as other wrenching cries and sobs pierced the air. And still people kept coming.

It took time for everyone to assemble. Standing in the cold, we were a solemn sight. Heavily armed stone-faced guards mercilessly prodded us, shoving us as they displayed their batons.

Loud protesting, terrible cries and moans came from all directions, but no one listened or cared; it all fell on deaf ears. My sister and I witnessed all of this without understanding the immense significance and horror of the situation.

It felt unseasonably cold, like a late autumn day. We could hear our own sorry steps as we shuffled along; the town centre once bustling with everyday activities was now silenced as this forced evacuation unfolded in plain sight.

Then we started to walk. As we distanced ourselves from the town of Edineţi, we knew that our beautiful childhood days of playing in the beautiful parks full of trees would forever remain just a cherished memory, never to return.

We realized even at the beginning of the march that when being made to walk for days on end, no matter how small a package one caries, it eventually becomes an enormously heavy load. As we marched along, many of us discarded some of our belongings to lighten our loads, making it easier to continue our desperate march to the unknown.

On the march, attending to our bodily needs could only be done with great difficulty. We had to squat, with one person shielding the other, and then we'd rush back to join the column — all under the watchful, impassive eyes of the Romanian soldiers walking alongside us, guarding our group in case anyone tried to flee.

The weather stayed exceptionally wet and very cold for the time of year, probably the coldest for many years. Roads, which were mainly dirt roads, were extremely muddy due to the never-ending rains. Enormous effort was required just to lift our legs from the mud for the next step, even for young limbs. Our footwear was caked instantly in the mud. Walking slowed down to a mere amble. Days turned to nights, and still we continued walking.

People pleaded with the guards to be allowed to rest when night approached, even just on the side of the road, but they had their orders; the march continued relentlessly.

Nights were particularly challenging. When the weather cleared, we saw nocturnal birds, mainly owls and bats, fluttering above us, and we soon realized they were dangerous if they landed in someone's hair. It was horrible getting a bat out of someone's hair. Frequent melancholic hooting sounds made by owls was enough to frighten even the bravest of us. I cannot remember encountering any larger animals, possibly because the sheer size of our column of humanity frightened them from getting close to us.

We noticed that the guards changed daily, but for us there was no rest and no relief from constant walking. I shall never forget the feeling of utter hopelessness that engulfed us continuously. We just wanted to be allowed to sit somewhere for a while, but it was not allowed. We kept walking.

It was then I realized that I could actually walk with my eyes closed, sleep and walk at the same time. To this day I still wonder how I stayed in an upright position all those endless hours, nights and days.

It soon became evident that our guards were immovable, and their plan was to cause us as much additional discomfort as possible. This march was calculated to annihilate as many of us as quickly as possible without firing a single shot. People were dropping where they stood from sheer exhaustion. Unable to continue, hungry, cold and desperate. Those who fell were left to die, and the rest of us were helpless, horrified onlookers. We could not help but wonder what fate awaited each of us.

Dirt from our endless march had by then become encrusted on our skin. Our faces had lost all expression. What drove us to keep walking and stay upright I still don't know. But we kept our fierce will to survive.

The following incident will remain etched in my mind for the rest of my life.

After days of marching, my father managed to pass the word around to everyone in the column, person by person, asking people to stop. They did. He then approached the soldiers at the head of the column. He stood in front of them, fearless, pleading for compassion, for some semblance of human feeling, to allow us to stop when night approached.

While he faced them, the soldiers had their weapons trained directly on his chest. We waited, unable to breathe, in stark fear, our hearts beating furiously and anticipating the worst, hoping desperately he would be spared. He succeeded, and his request was granted. From that time on, we were allowed to rest wherever we happened to be as night approached, whether we were close to farms, forests or towns. It was a small, important triumph for us, and my father was henceforth regarded by all as a brave saviour. He had taken the risk knowing perfectly well he could easily have been shot for his audacity.

As dawn arrived each day, we continued walking. We were bedraggled, dirty, stiff and tired, yet still we continued for what seemed to be an eternity. At least we could now rest at night.

While we walked, villagers would come out to the road, some out of curiosity and pity, with carafes of water, bread and cheese, which we could buy or barter for. It had to be done swiftly, so as not to anger the soldiers who were under orders to keep us marching.

Periodically, guards would distribute dry bread rations. It was always old bread chunks and little else, handed out quickly so as not to hold up the march. Sometimes we came across fields of growing beets, which we pulled out of the ground and ate raw, skin included; we considered it a feast. We also came upon a farm that had a stack of pressed round blocks of dried sunflower seeds still in their shells, obviously intended as animal fodder. They were edible, though, and the seeds were almost a treat.

During our march we searched for anything that would allow us to clean our teeth, and we eventually discovered that ash could help. Using ash collected from various places on our way, we rubbed our teeth and gums with a finger covered with ash. It was gritty, unpleasant and it dried the inside of our mouths, but there was no alternative.

Each day saw more people drop only to be left where they fell. It is hard to describe our state. Our shoes had begun to fall apart. Some dumped their disintegrated footwear quickly, winding rags made out of anything they could find — shirts, sheets, pillowcases — around their swollen, tired feet.

Although it felt like such a long time had passed since the day we started our march, it may well have been days or weeks only; we had lost all sense of time. We stopped in a town near a river in Ukraine. We were mercifully allowed to rest in what looked like a hastily abandoned place. Buildings stood vacant, not a soul in sight; all one could hear inside the dwellings was the wind noisily blowing, whistling, invading through porous walls.

Silence prevailed throughout the place; it had a disturbing, mournful feel, even eerie. We were taken to a large building, which could have been a hall of some sort and was filled with as many people as it could accommodate. There, we waited for the next orders we knew would come.

Hungry, frightened and in deep despair, my sweet sister, Dorica, disappeared from our resting place. I took it upon myself to find her, looking everywhere — I searched for her among vacant dwellings and along the roads, hoping she had just strayed and somehow lost her way. Desperate and almost close to giving up, I finally found her at the edge of the river. She was hysterical, sobbing as she told me she could no longer live this way, that she'd had as much as she could take and did not want to continue in misery but wanted to end it all by throwing herself into the river. Neither of us could swim.

She was just sixteen years old and could not summon the courage to go on. It took a lot of tearful persuasion from me — I don't know exactly what I said to her or where I summoned the strength to convince her not to give up and to stay with us. I implored and I begged, said everything I could think of to convince her, trying desperately to make her understand that somehow we would get through and survive. I told her how much she was loved, needed, how important it was for us, her family, to be together to support each other. I tried to make her understand how painful it would be for our parents, who were already suffering so much, if she insisted on going through with her plan.

It was one of the most heartbreaking situations for both of us. We clung to each other and sobbed for what seemed like an eternity, until at last she agreed to return with me, to face our destiny together.

We decided not to tell our parents about this incident. Neither of us wanted to burden them with what had transpired at that river's edge — my father and Ethel had enough to bear. Instead, we told them that Dorica had lost her way and had been wandering around trying to find us. In fact, she was a lost soul in more ways than one, ready to give up.

Not long after the frightening incident with my sister, destiny sadly released her anyway. Lack of proper nourishment, poor sanitary conditions, plus an onslaught of vermin were taking their toll on everyone. Dorica had contracted the dreaded disease of typhus and fell desperately ill.

She required immediate medical attention and rest, but neither were available. My father begged the authorities to take pity on a young girl and help her find a doctor. The guards suggested we leave her with them, saying she would be hospitalized. But we knew what that meant — she would be abused then murdered.

The disease racked her body; in her unhygienic state, with no food and already weak, Dorica had no way to fight the infection. All we could do was be with her to soothe her feverish brow, support her poor dehydrated body. We stood by helplessly watching her condition deteriorate by the minute, unable to do anything to save her. She died in my father's arms, the three of us with her.

There was no possibility of a funeral; people were dropping dead where they fell and were abandoned to the elements. My father decided that he and I would somehow bury my sister ourselves. We strayed from our column, and he carried her poor body to the site of a small hill. The two of us used our bare hands and some sticks and stones found on the road to dig a hole that would hold her. He said Kaddish, the prayer for the dead, and after that we wrapped her clothed body in a sheet, covered her remains with dirt as best we could and walked away.

No one should ever have to make that kind of brutal decision to bury and abandon a loved one — a cherished child and beloved sister who in normal times would have had a promising life in front of her.

I remember the awful pain I felt at the thought of never seeing my sister again. I did not want to leave without her. Nothing could console me. I wept for her, for myself, for my parents, for the situation that brought us to this moment, for not being able to help my family, for the deep sense of loss I felt. The pain, anger and frustration would not leave me, and I still feel it to this very day.

It was then, faced with this painful loss, that I renewed my resolution to do my utmost to live, to help my parents as much as possible and to survive, no matter what hardships I had to endure.

Much later, when we could think clearly about our situation, we took solace in the fact that at least her remains would not be treated like garbage. The anguish we all suffered took its toll on each of us — our only consolation was the knowledge that she was finally at rest and forever free of persecution.

Unexpected Help

I do not recall crossing the river from that town, but cross we must have, as I do remember reaching the outskirts of a town on the other side called Moghilev-Podolsk (now Mohyliv-Podilskyi, Ukraine), where the convoy finally paused. Dwellings of sorts were found for us, which might have been vacant army barracks.

The march continued after a few days' respite. We started to get the impression that no one knew what to do with us. The guards might have been waiting for further orders, or perhaps, for them, too many of us still refused to die. For us, there was no end in sight. Imprinted in my mind is the sight of so many people with their feet wound in rags, shuffling along, willing themselves to remain upright, desperate to endure.

Eventually, we stopped when we arrived at the small town of Murafa, part of which would become a ghetto. All of us who had survived the long march were now a wreck — weak, dirty, exhausted from the inhuman treatment we had endured. How could anyone have contemplated escape? I have since learned, to my amazement, that in total there were about 150 concentration camps and ghettos holding Romanian Jews in the region of Transnistria, the name for the surrounding area where we were finally allowed to stop.

We had no food, since we had already bartered every possible item we possessed for food from farmers on our march, and received very little for it. We knew we had to have some source of income. One of the villagers outside the ghetto in Murafa with whom we bartered suggested I come to mind her very young child in her home. She proposed to pay me with supplies and produce.

I was young and could sneak out of the ghetto without being noticed. We needed food to survive and working at whatever came my way — housework, fieldwork, babysitting, knitting — was the only way to get it. The school year under the Soviet regime had helped me understand the Ukrainian language, as it is similar to Russian.

Working for farmers in nearby villages was undoubtedly dangerous, but I had little to lose. Besides, a lot depended on being able to help my parents; this was not courage, it was desperation. With this in mind, I was ready for what had to be done.

One day, while returning to the ghetto from the village, tired after a long day, I encountered two drunks, who very quickly realized I was Jewish, considered an inmate. Hatred of Jews was deep-rooted. They yelled for me to stop. Like a fool, I stopped instead of running away. Like lightning, before I realized their intention, they were upon me and blows from both of them started raining on me. They used their arms and fists to beat me and their feet to kick me. Landing in the dirt at their feet, I lay there as they kept on pummelling me until I was doubled up with pain, bleeding from all the blows. They made sure I understood that if I tried to get out again, the same treatment would await me.

I was probably lucky to escape with a beating from two drunks, who were so intoxicated they had difficulty even standing. Had they been sober, it could have been a lot worse. I got to my feet after they had staggered away, my body in terrible pain, heart beating wildly. I staggered back to the ghetto, where my shocked father and Ethel took care of me. They soothed me and cleaned all my cuts. They promised that soon our misery would end, that life would return to normal and we would be free once more.

For me, there was no escaping working in the village; it was our only way to get food. We put together a plan whereby I would be disguised as a peasant girl. Somehow we acquired a proper peasant skirt and top, along with a head scarf. This outfit completed my transformation, enabling me to continue working in the village. We fervently hoped my new outfit would avoid future dangerous incidents.

My daily walks to the village resumed, and one night, I agreed to stay overnight for additional pay to care for a woman's baby while she went out of the village. Before she left, she showed me a large alcove above her coal stove where I could sleep, a warm spot since the stove was in daily use.

I settled down for the night after attending to her child, who was sleeping peacefully nearby. Lulled by the warmth of the alcove, I fell into a deep sleep only to wake with a start: someone was in the house, a man who by his behaviour was clearly not a stranger to the owner. Familiar with the surroundings, he came directly to the alcove where she probably also slept. The stranger, obviously looking for the woman, found me instead. He started groping me, ready to pounce, his intentions clear. I cried, pleading with him to stop, telling him I was just a child and yelling loud enough to wake the baby, who mercifully did wake and also started screaming. The man left without hurting me — only frightening me close to death. He had obviously been drinking, as I had smelled alcohol on his breath. When the woman returned the following day and heard about the incident, she calmly shrugged it off, obviously not thinking it was important, nor did she care. It was the last time I took on work from her.

Many other villagers were in need of workers to help them. They were hard-working farmers, and I was a willing worker: harvesting vegetables, picking fruit, doing housework and, if they happened to have yarn, even knitting items for them.

Life continued in this manner, working every day. In the evenings, I would make my way back with whatever I had managed to collect as payment. All that mattered was survival. I continued working for different farmers, good people grateful to have an additional pair of hands. I earned their respect and just enough fresh food to keep us alive. It was a distressing time for all of us, yet we never stopped hoping that somehow we would one day be safe once again.

Our unsanitary conditions brought bedbugs, lice and various illnesses. When we were lucky to find kerosene, we used to pour it in water then wash my hair to get rid of lice. It was a painful way to rid ourselves of vermin. Eventually, the infestation was so bad that we had to shave my head — nothing else would help. I wrapped a scarf around my head to cover the shame I felt at having no hair for a time. Of course, the knowledge that it would grow back was consoling.

I always looked forward to spending time alone with my father. Those were the most precious times for me. We would walk around the ghetto in the evening when the sun set and the skies lit up with stars. This had special meaning for me. He would name the stars, telling me about the Milky Way and all the constellations he knew so well, assuring me that the sky really enveloped the entire world. He would assure me that our ordeal would soon be over and that we would resume our lives in total freedom, just like all humans in the rest of the world.

As time passed, everyone's clothing was in tatters, and we were lucky to have anything to wear to cover our emaciated bodies — like all the people in the ghetto, we had become skeletal. Those who had shoes kept stitching or binding them with rope or straw, whatever they could find to hold the soles together. Many of us could no longer wear shoes because our feet were badly swollen, covered with horrible open sores. We found a way to bandage our feet with rags made from torn-up garments, bedclothes or even straw. The ghetto was an awful sight, hard to forget.

～

Help for me came from an unexpected source early in 1944. Unbeknownst to me, Father had found out that representatives from international aid organizations and Jewish organizations, building on earlier negotiations by Jewish leaders, were working with Romanian leaders to receive permission to secure passage to Palestine for orphaned children. He had immediately entered my name on a list of orphans to be sent out of Transnistria. I was told by my father that a Jewish organization in the United States had negotiated with Romania, that large sums of money had been discussed and, in time, permission had been obtained to allow orphaned Jewish children to be sent to safety. The understanding was that children would be allowed to leave under certain conditions and find ways and transport to get to Palestine.

At first the news made me sad, and I rebelled at the thought of leaving my father and Ethel alone. I could not imagine leaving my family and worried they would be unable to sustain themselves without me. What would happen to them? That's when my father told me that he knew we were in a horrible situation and that anything could happen. But here was a chance for me to escape, survive and be free once again. No one knew what was in store for anyone — this opportunity had presented itself and I should take it, he said. Besides, by leaving for Palestine and freedom, at least one of us would survive. I had to take the chance, but it was heartbreaking leaving them behind.

Some time went by, and we had little communication from any organization. I wondered if it was just a promise that would perhaps not materialize. But then the news came that I had been accepted. My father again insisted that I go, regardless of how I felt about leaving them. Strangely, although I was devastated and emotional about leaving them, the hope of a normal life was irresistible and I agreed to leave.

Soon a cattle truck arrived to take me and others to a centre where transport would be provided for us to our destination. We were taken across the river and had not travelled far before we stopped and were met by a delegation of women who were members of a Zionist organization. We were taken to a hall where there were facilities available for us to wash, and food and some clothing were provided.

We then boarded a cattle train, with no seats and with its floors strewn with straw. We were on the way to a city in Romania I knew as Kishinev (Chişinău, now in Moldova), where we would wait for transport that would take us to Palestine.

On our arrival, we were met by a delegation of Jewish folks who in turn took us to what may have been a school hall. There, families awaited us who would take us into their homes and foster us until transport became available for our final destination. Young children were the first to be chosen. I was sixteen, and many others my age waited a while longer to be fostered. Finally I was approached by a family of three adults, two sisters and a brother who were I think in their late forties, and they took me into their care for the duration of my stay.

I was certainly lucky. The Hirsh family was kind and understanding. They handled my fragile state with the utmost care. In the warmth of their home and with their gracious, compassionate attitude toward me, I began to heal in many ways. They were gentle people who, from the start, treated me like a member of their family with absolutely no reservations. To them I will forever be grateful.

We waited for word of our departure, which kept being delayed. I found out later that while we were waiting to leave for Palestine, the Jewish organizations never ceased their negotiations for our passage out of Romania. They met with constant delays and resistance. The ongoing war did nothing to relieve the situation.

We were then moved to Iaşi, yet another city in Romania. Parting from the family who fostered me was painfully sad. We went through the same process of being fostered in Iaşi, taken in by local families, who would care for us until the long-awaited ships arrived. Rumours abounded about the war being near its end, but no one knew for certain. For a time, it was just rumours.

It was 1945 by the time the ships were in port waiting for us. We had heard chilling news about one ship the previous summer — after the ship of refugees had sailed, it had been torpedoed and sunk in the Black Sea, killing three hundred people on board, including children.

Eventually, two ships were secured to transport some of us to Palestine via Turkey. Each ship could take only a certain number of passengers, leaving the others behind. When the first group of children left, the rest of us were envious.

My turn came in May of 1945. After months of delay due to lack of availability of a transport, we were finally being sent to Palestine. We were first put on a cattle train to Turkey, where we boarded a merchant ship. Our passage to freedom was about to become reality. It would take two days for the small ship to sail to Palestine. We were packed in tightly, but we gladly endured the discomfort in the knowledge we would soon be free.

Freedom to Heal

It finally happened — I had arrived in Palestine. I had survived! It was the month of May, just after the end of World War II in Europe. Emotionally a wreck, teary-eyed, yet hopeful to start my new life's adventure, I arrived at Atlit, a former British army camp in the port of Haifa that was now a detention camp that held refugees.

The camp was large; there were some administrative brick buildings and temporary housing for the refugees like us who were arriving in large numbers to seek sanctuary. On arrival, each one of us was registered and interviewed to supply detailed personal information, which would be entered on a list to be published in all newspapers. About fifteen people were housed in each of the temporary structures. We were given reasonable food and the daily necessities of life. Hebrew lessons soon followed, enabling us to communicate with those in charge, who spoke mostly Hebrew, probably also Yiddish.

We were what they called "displaced persons," since we had no documents to prove who we were. For now we were being kept at Atlit and learning Hebrew, and it seemed like in time we would eventually be placed on communal farms, kibbutzim.

I was feeling a mix of emotions — happy to be free from persecution but missing my father and stepmother. Leaving them was a most painful wrench for me, made worse by the knowledge that I might not see them again. I never gave up looking for my family. I kept asking about them through the International Red Cross, which specialized in tracing services after the war. It was a lengthy, difficult process hampered by language difficulties, red tape, problems obtaining details from the Soviet Union, which was mostly uncooperative. To my great joy and relief, my family was eventually located. They had survived and now lived in Kiev. As soon as I had their address, we started to correspond (neither of us had access to a telephone). It was a great relief for both my parents and me just to know the other had survived — there was always the hope we would see each other someday.

Atlit was a busy place, and the organizers did a good job informing us of what we could expect. A mixture of all kinds of people bustled about in the camp, including members of the Haganah, a tough, undercover, no-nonsense military movement that used violent tactics to deal with border skirmishes. These dedicated, brave individuals were anxious to recruit new members for their cause. They were determined to protect the country against hostilities in any way possible — resisting against both Arab groups and the British, who refused to allow in more Jewish refugees and were deporting Jewish immigrants who had already arrived.

Members of the Haganah approached many of us refugees to persuade us to enlist, and one of them approached me as well. Having just arrived, I was trying hard to heal, and I declined, certainly not ready to undertake any kind of undercover activities. I don't think the members of the Haganah understood my emotional state and what I was going through. They simply needed new members for their organization, but I was unable to contemplate such a life. Besides, having lost all those years, I was longing to get back to normal, peaceful living. First, I needed to focus on my education, which had been so abruptly stopped by Nazi occupation. My ambition was to try to put everything that had happened behind me as soon as I could, and embrace life again.

∼

With all I'd been through, I forgot we had relatives who had settled in Palestine years earlier — my late mother's brothers. One day, about two weeks after arriving in Atlit, a call came for me to present myself to the administrative office. Unexpectedly, a surprise awaited me a relative! Having read the published list of refugees, my mother's brother Seymour Maimon arrived, intent on finding me. I was overjoyed to see him, and memories drifted back of a fun-loving uncle, who when my sister and I were little always found time to spend amusing us.

I was grateful that he had sought me out. He wanted to know as much as possible about the dreadful atrocities we had experienced, everything about the years after the deportation from Romania. As he listened quietly to my story, I filled him on details of the Holocaust years the best I could. He told me how happy he was I had escaped. He realized all the years I had been denied schooling. Having made some prior enquiries, he found a college that would suit my needs and came prepared to take me there to see what he could do to get me accepted. I agreed to go with him in the hope that I would be suitable for the program the college was running.

After a series of formalities, my uncle completed all the necessary documentation for me to formally leave the refugee camp. We acquired a form that confirmed my immigrant status, name, age and origin. After verifying my identity, I happily left the sanctuary of Atlit with my uncle, on my way to a new life. During the early years of the Holocaust, the Nazis had taken possession of or destroyed every single document any of us had, including birth certificates, ownership documents, identity papers, my parents' marriage certificate. Now the only way I could prove my identity was this new document from Atlit.

In 1945 in Palestine, which had been under a British mandate since 1920, British soldiers seemed to be everywhere, supposedly to keep the peace. They imposed nightly curfews and patrolled the streets. The Jews in Palestine tolerated them, only just. It was difficult to admire them — they were a necessary evil.

My uncle took me to his home, a small apartment in the heart of Tel Aviv where he lived with his wife, Gusty. I met my aunt for the first time — Austrian by birth, she was charming, kind and tactful. I don't remember what language we spoke together; it may have been Yiddish, as she did not speak Romanian. My uncle outlined his plans for my immediate future. The agricultural college for girls had been established by the government to fill the needs of refugees who found themselves in the same position as me. It was administered by a team of retired teachers, who were also in charge, and it was run as a working farm. Attached to the farm was a citrus grove, where oranges, grapefruit, lemons and more grew in profusion and were then harvested and sold.

I stayed with my uncle and aunt a few days before I was taken to Rehovot and the agricultural college in nearby Ayanot. To my great joy, I was accepted there after being interviewed by a group of teachers and informed in detail what the college stood for and how it worked. I was to be given board and lodging for a period of two years, in which time I would spend mornings working the farm in various roles. Each student would be allocated specific jobs — farming, animal care, kitchen duties, cleaning, picking citrus in season, gardening or serving food at mealtimes. My jobs would be cleaning and citrus picking. Afternoons were strictly for studying. Our curriculum consisted of Hebrew, history, science, geography and math. The idea was to cram two years of learning into one year, thus getting as reasonable an education as possible.

It took some time for me to recover from all I had been through, and the manual work was varied and hard, but it was also enjoyable and the school was an amazing experience. I do not recall how many of us there were — there might have been 120 or more students. Accommodation was shared, with four girls per room. The showers were located in an enormous room divided into many open cubicles and affording absolutely no privacy, which took some adjusting to.

Breakfast was available early, at probably 5:00 a.m. or even earlier. If you missed it you went without. Lunch was a spartan affair, consisting of healthy, good food mostly grown on the farm. Dinner was available in the early evening and was usually a hot stew. No one went hungry. We had free time in the evenings and usually congregated in small groups with friends we quickly made, using our time to learn Hebrew songs or do our daily homework revisions.

Saturdays were always special — no work or school except for those of us whose turn it was to do weekend shift work. Everyone took turns at shift work sooner or later. On these days off, usually Friday evenings and Saturdays, we would gather to socialize in the hall that served as the dining room. Despite it being an all-girls school, there were some men in charge of specific heavy equipment and implements normally used in farm work. These workers would offer to take us out on Saturdays in their farm trucks to show us the surrounding area, which was just what we needed.

On one such Saturday out in a truck, we encountered many kibbutzim. The entire area we visited was verdant, lush and extremely well kept, and teeming with youngsters dedicated to kibbutz living. I got to know some of them. I admired their dedication to work, but I also saw they had a casual attitude and the freedom to do absolutely anything they wanted.

One weekend we came upon what looked like a gated establishment. The driver decided we should see what was behind these gates, so we drove in slowly, but before we knew it we were greeted by a barrage of stones from yelling, enraged men. Clusters of earth and other projectiles were raining on us from all directions. We soon discovered that we'd stumbled upon a group of ultra-religious Jews for whom Shabbat was a most sacred day, when no one leaves the compound and no cars were allowed in or out. I found out later that some very religious Jews also declared themselves army dissidents and did not allow their sons and daughters to enlist. We had to leave quickly.

On other Saturday outings we met with young people eager to help us assimilate, mostly kibbutz youth. We learned to dance the hora properly and had great fun in the process, getting to know each other better and enjoying life.

Throughout the two years at the college, each one of us progressed, enabling us to learn our chosen subjects, providing us the knowledge we needed. I became aware that both the government and our teachers were grooming us for kibbutz life, and although some girls did indeed choose kibbutz life, it was not my choice to be a kibbutznik.

We were young and full of hope, dreaming of what we would do when our two years were over. No matter how hard the work, it was healing. Learning a new language and the other high school subjects contributed to instilling new values and self-assurance. I felt lucky to be in the college and receiving schooling; those two years in Ayanot were instrumental in rebuilding my life.

New Ventures

In 1947, after I had completed college, my uncle Seymour offered me work. He had established a successful import-export business and had an office. When he asked me if I would like to work for him in his office, I agreed. He also told me that if I wanted I could take an evening course in commerce, which he suggested would help me in the future. I enrolled in a night school and learned touch typing, shorthand and office routines.

Working during the day and studying in the evening took a lot of initiative and concentration. The teachers were good — they knew how to get the best out of all of us. In no time, I mastered touch typing, which is taught by memorizing the letters on the typewriter layout until one is able to find any letter without looking down.

We then moved to shorthand, for which there existed a set lot of symbols to memorize, allowing us to quickly write a substituted condensed written word when transcribing a dictated letter. At that time, it was a popular way of transcribing a letter so that the contents could be typed later. At the end of my course, I earned my diploma, which gave me a much-needed boost.

I then took a three-month course, two hours per evening, in the Berlitz School of Languages. Our teacher introduced himself in English, the language I was there to learn, and as far as I could tell he spoke no other language. The Berlitz method teaches new languages without ever translating words, using only the language a person is learning to immerse students in it. It was not easy, but I liked learning languages and concentrated on what I had to do, giving it my best.

At the end of the course, I was able to converse in a very broken English. I shook hands with the teacher, who surprised me by speaking Hebrew! I could cheerfully have kicked him then! He advised me to register at a library, take out a book in English and read it, if possible, aloud.

Following his advice, I borrowed the book *Rebecca* by Daphne du Maurier and read it cover to cover, underlying unfamiliar words by pencil with a dictionary at the ready. It took me a long time to read the book, but it was a big help. In time, I became proficient in English.

～

Israel declared its independence after the British mandate expired; the year was 1948, and Israel was at war. Bordered by hostile Arab countries such as Lebanon and Jordan, the new State of Israel issued a call to arms compelling all citizens ages eighteen and over to enlist in the army for two years.

Full of enthusiasm, happy to serve, I presented myself to the recruiting centre for a mandatory health examination and various tests. This opened up an opportunity for me to become part of the people, a citizen of Israel and no longer just an immigrant.

I was issued military gear consisting of a full khaki uniform, shirt, skirt, trousers and heavy footwear; a folding camp bed; and a floppy hat, a must in the sunny Israeli climate.

Following an initial examination, I was interviewed at length by a panel of expert recruiting officers to properly assess my capabilities and army potential. Afterwards, I was chosen to train in communication skills. I commenced an intensive three-month course, which, when completed, would qualify me to be sent to active duty.

It was still the era of Morse code, which required field telephone installation, cable laying, bunker communication expertise and codes.

That is what I had to learn to be able to take on the communication position. Communication was done by wiring from post to post and by using a hand tapping device sending coded messages daily; we also learned a list of codes used in emergencies.

Each day started with exercises, and the training was merciless. While laying cables, we carried heavy backpacks containing tools, necessary equipment and rations. We learned to connect cables on barren, uneven terrain by crawling under wire fences at night. Instructions issued were to be precisely executed, and gender was no consideration — this was the army and there was much work to be done in a small amount of time.

Standards were high. Everything had to fall into place like clock-work. We were being trained to be soldiers, learning how to march with precision, over and over until the sergeant in charge was totally satisfied with our performance. Our lecturers were mostly Israelis who were nicknamed *sabras*, known in English as prickly pears, a cactus plant that is prickly on the outside and sweet on the inside. There were inevitable clashes between recruits and lecturers, with their unique no-nonsense attitude. When not in lectures or training, we had very little time off, but the facilities were the best and the food excellent.

After three months of training, which felt more like three years, I successfully graduated and was then attached to a regiment stationed in the Negev Desert, the southern region of the country, which at the time was barren — just sand and stone.

Here, I learned how to adapt my newly learned craft to army requirements. Women were not sent to the front, nor did we stand guard at the borders. Instead, we were the front-line support. But each of us was still issued an automatic weapon and ammunition, which we were trained to use — loading, unloading, cleaning, oiling, maintaining, dissembling and assembling the weapon in record time. I have to admit that during my army years I did not fire the gun, not even once. It was part of our uniform, carried on the shoulder in case of an emergency.

Our sleeping quarters were in huge dugouts, which smelled of fresh earth and were uncomfortable even with our folding canvas beds. I felt like I was sleeping on a narrow stretcher, but we were young and adapted easily. Rations were adequate; no luxuries, only what was strictly necessary.

Standard cooking facilities were unavailable in the field, so cooking was done on small portable gas cookers. Our meals included milk, fruit, vegetables, bread and for protein, sardines. Not in my wildest dreams had I imagined that it was possible to turn the lowly tinned sardines into a variety of dishes; they were offered to us in the form of soup, stews, croquettes, sandwiches and salads. Thankfully no one was allergic to sardines, although at times we were almost certain we'd all end up looking and smelling like some type of sardine!

It was also a time when everyone smoked cigarettes. Smoking looked enticing and seemed ever so sophisticated. I watched my comrades skilfully hold a cigarette between two fingers while puffing away. I longed to be exactly like them. Cigarettes were issued monthly by our field canteen. After obtaining my ration, I decided to practise (thankfully in private). I found a spot at the back of some tents, but try as I might, I could not master the art. Smoking made me horribly ill, and I gave up. Obviously unsophisticated and admitting defeat, I returned the coveted smokes to the canteen, where to my delight they were exchanged, no question asked, for monthly issues of chocolates, which helped turn me into a sworn chocoholic instead.

During these army years, I formed true friendships. When not on duty, we would gather outside on the Sabbath when night fell, forming a wide circle in the sand under beautiful clear starry skies. We chatted, sang patriotic songs, danced the hora, enjoyed the warm weather and shamelessly flirted with handsome soldiers.

After the end of the war, Israel was flooded with immigrants, many of whom, like me, were Holocaust survivors. Despite the care lavished on us and tactful handling, many survivors bore their years of suffering with great difficulty. Unable to adapt to normal life, they ended up in clinical care, and some even in institutions.

I was without a doubt one of the lucky ones, adjusting well to a new life. Also, I found the army liberating in a sense — it gave me a feeling of belonging, of being needed and useful, and it strengthened and shaped the person I am today. For me, those two years spent in the Negev serving the country will always bring back memories of learned discipline, doing a great, useful task, happy days filled with the natural beauty of our surroundings and the wonderful, new, lasting friendships. We all shared the same love for the country.

When our two-year service was over, we were discharged, and each of us received a medal and the country's thanks. Our final instructions were that although our two-year service had come to an end, we were required to present ourselves to army headquarters once a year until our single status changed, which I did until 1951.

After I was discharged from the army, I rented a room I had previously stayed in. I felt like I was now back to facing reality — which meant finding work. Scanning daily ads in the paper, I found an advertisement for a secretary to the airport manager, which sounded interesting. I called for an appointment and arranged an interview with the airport manager, Mr. Zur, a few days later.

Mr. Zur turned out to be an affable, informal person. He told me that despite the size of the airport, he was kept busy running it. At the time, Lod Airport (later renamed Ben Gurion) was not large and certainly not yet international, but there was air traffic of mainly small- and medium-sized planes.

The interview went well. After checking my credentials, impressed by my knowledge of English, even though heavily accented, he told me that every secretary he employed in the past left to marry. He said, "Can you promise me that if I employ you, you will not marry and then leave too?" I was not sure if he was joking or trying to put me at ease. I did not have a boyfriend then, so I could truthfully tell him I had no such plans and would be happy to have the job.

Mr. Zur was a kind boss. He took his time explaining what was expected of me. He held a private pilot's licence and owned a small aircraft, which he frequently used for business trips. During the time

I worked for him, he took me for spins in his small craft.

My job was interesting — answering calls, typing, taking letters, issuing permits and generally taking care of the office. Something different each day. It was Tel Aviv's major airport and had one kosher restaurant in the terminal building, owned by a Mr. Levi. Daily arrivals and departures took place on the same floor. The restaurant was also a place where airport personnel frequently came for a cup of coffee, a bite to eat or just for a chat with friends. This became my daily routine, going downstairs at lunch time for a snack, always chocolate. It was about all I could afford.

One day, sitting quietly at one of the restaurant tables, a customs officer I knew made his way to my table accompanied by a man I'd seen around but did not know. He introduced me to his friend, a South African flight engineer named William (Bill) Esterhuizen. I'd actually seen Bill before once or twice and liked what I saw — this tall, fair, handsome man made a good impression on me. He obviously felt the same way about me, and thus started the beginning of our getting to know each other and our courtship.

At the time, Bill was on contract to an Israeli recruiting firm, which in time became part of El Al airline. Israel employed aviation specialists like Bill from various countries to train Israelis in fully servicing their different kinds of aircraft and help establish the new Israeli airline.

I remember my first date with Bill: we were invited to a Purim party, the first I'd ever been to and most probably his first too. We spent a joyful evening among friends. We soon got to know each other better, meeting as often as we could and spending our free time walking around Tel Aviv. Sometimes we went to the beach, where I would suntan while Bill swam. We talked a lot, and aside from getting to know each other, I also improved my English. Tel Aviv's entertainment area had many coffee shops, where light classical violin music played in the afternoons and where theatregoers stopped by in the evenings; these were romantic venues for couples, and we frequented them often.

Six months into our courtship, he proposed to me. Some months later, in August 1951, the two of us and our two witnesses travelled to the British consulate in Haifa; an official there, having received our prior request, married us. I was twenty-four years old, and Bill was twenty-eight. We had a reception for about forty friends at a friend's apartment. At that time, food essentials in Israel were rationed. Bill took a flight to Cyprus, bought supplies, including ingredients needed for a wedding cake, which someone baked for us, and cold cuts to serve to our guests with salads and various drinks.

Now that Bill was a married man, El Al provided us with an apartment in a high-rise building owned by them situated in the town of Bat Yam, close to the beach on the Mediterranean Sea. This building was eventually entirely occupied by foreign employees of the airline, from different countries around the world. We soon became a close community and made many friends, often having pleasant evening barbecues on the beach.

In June 1952, our first child was born, a boy we named Laurence. This was the first grandchild for Bill's parents, and naturally they wanted to see him. The three of us took a trip to Springs, South Africa, to meet my in-laws and for them to see their first grandson, then just five months old. Meeting Bill's parents and three sisters was an emotional experience for me in so many ways. We visited with them for a short two weeks, and I enjoyed getting to know them, their warm-heartedness, their love for their only son evident in their reaction and acceptance of me. They were decent, loving people whose hospitality and kindness knew no limits. I took to them instantly, basking in the love they showed to the three of us. Leaving them to return to Israel saddened me. We said our goodbyes to Bill's family, who in that short time had become attached to their grandson and wished we did not have to leave.

No more than two years later, in 1954, Bill's contract with the firm expired. Our son was now almost two years old, and we packed our belongings and said goodbye to our many friends. We were given the option to go to any country of our choice, so we chose South Africa — mainly because of Bill's family but also because he loved his home country. Our intention was to make it our forever home. After applying for immigrant status and going through the usual red tape, I received the papers allowing me to enter the country.

Before we moved to South Africa, I did my best to get more information about the country and its various problems of inequality, the unjust government in power. It was not easy for me to adapt, since their ideology was completely foreign to me. Neither Bill nor I were politically minded, and I slowly learned the laws of the country and did my best to adapt, made easier with the support of Bill's family and knowing that this country would now be our home.

Life in South Africa

On arrival, we rented a house in a lovely area of Johannesburg called Primrose. One year later we became proud owners of a newly constructed home in another suburb called Hurlyvale, close to schools and not far from a shopping area. While all this was happening, Bill accepted a position with the country's airline.

A year after our arrival in South Africa, we welcomed our second son, Mark, and three years later we were blessed with one more child, a son we named William.

We slowly built for ourselves and our children a life we wanted in a country with a warm to moderate climate, good schools, with family nearby, new friends and good neighbours. We enjoyed living in South Africa, in the newly formed community of our choice. For a time, while our children were too young for school, I was a stay-at-home mom, making sure our children were involved in various activities. As our children grew, we carpooled with our immediate neighbours, taking turns to get them to school.

Eventually, Bill accepted a flight engineer's position with Luxair, a Luxembourg-based airline. Due to political pressure, the country's airline was not permitted to fly through most South African air spaces during the years of its apartheid regime. Luxair's partnership with a South African airline enabled South Africa to resume its normal travel to European countries. It also meant Bill would be away from home frequently, which was a difficult adjustment for us.

Throughout the years, I learned a bit about Black South Africans and their struggles, mainly through housemaids in our employ. Housework was a common occupation for women from the smaller villages who had little education, since other employment opportunities were almost non-existent. Housework allowed them to earn a living and brought them from rural areas into the cities. I learned of their issues with lack of education and training, and about their unique culture and traditions.

As our children blossomed and grew, we travelled all over the country to experience its breathtaking beauty. On more than one vacation we ventured to Mozambique's Parque Flores, a fishing and boating resort. Our sons enjoyed boating and swimming and the camaraderie of other young people their age. We mostly camped, and on one of our vacations we acquired a tent, thinking it would afford us more sleeping space.

The first night that Bill and I decided to sleep in the new tent, we had our sleeping bags ready when night arrived. It took me a while to fall asleep, not being an avid camper, but eventually I dozed off. Suddenly I heard what sounded like a crunching noise but could not find the source of the sound. I decided to wake Bill, who was a sound sleeper. At first, he could not decide where the noise was coming from, but he found it soon enough. The culprit was a bug almost the size of a loonie — it was systematically crunching the ceiling of our tent, obviously enjoying its meal!

My husband used heavy pliers to remove it and hopefully hasten its demise, but no hammering on the insect's shell or squeezing it could remove this insect. When he managed to persuade the critter to move, Bill picked it up and threw it as far as he could. We could not identify the culprit, so we named it the tent eater. This little episode was not a figment of our imagination — the proof of its presence was the sizable hole on our new tent's ceiling.

On one occasion we decided to spend our vacation in Durban, a seaside city in the province of Natal (now KwaZulu-Natal). It is called the garden province for its verdant lush fields and valleys. The province's long shoreline is on the Indian Ocean and borders Mozambique and Swaziland to the north, and Lesotho to the west.

When we told our housemaid at the time, Dora, of our vacation plans, thinking that she could take advantage of our time away — perhaps to go to visit her home for the duration — she told me she had never been to the coast and that to be able to see the ocean would be a dream come true for her. It was not easy, but I persuaded my husband to consider this and agree to invite Dora to accompany us on this vacation. Her joy when she learned that she could join us was truly rewarding.

We had rented a two-bedroom townhouse in a suburb close to the beach, and all of us were raring to go. All six of us, including our little dog, Gigi, piled into our station wagon and were on our way.

We were in Durban to enjoy its beautiful beaches — our plan was to spend as much time as possible worshipping the sun. But the problem of the apartheid era laws was staring us in the face — Black people, like our maid, were not permitted on these beaches. We were courting disaster; we felt powerless.

Dora made friends easily, and before we knew it, she had met and befriended some maids in the vicinity. She spent time with them whenever possible. She understood how essential it was to keep a low profile and avoid confrontation with the local police, so she hung around with us in the role of nanny, enjoying the ocean view from a distance. But we were all uneasy and contrite, unable to change the situation.

After a week of unease, embarrassment and tension, we realized that it was not a holiday for us or for her. In the end, with her consent and a sigh of relief, we took her to the train station, where we purchased a ticket enabling her to make her way to visit her own home and relative safety.

～

In 1960, I decided to apply for work at Nestlé when they advertised for some open positions. Nestlé had just acquired Crosse & Blackwell, a British firm that manufactured sauces and other products. I was accepted and trained to assist in their laboratory. One of my daily activities was preparing various products for daily testing and sampling; the one I liked best was Crosse & Blackwell's custard powder. I worked for Nestlé for a total of eighteen years, during which time they celebrated their anniversary of one hundred years in business in 1966.

I left my job at Nestlé to work in real estate for a friend who had opened a business and invited me to join her. She offered me half-days of office work and said, "You never know, you might even decide to sell properties one day."

One day when this friend was out of town for a short break, she remembered she had booked a house showing while she was away for a new property on ten acres of land. Unable to return in time, she asked me to do all the necessary preparation needed to show it: take photographs, write an ad, meet the seller and be there to show the house.

Since it was a first for me, I asked one of the agents to accompany me for the day to show the property. It was a well-built home on a large piece of land, in a new neighbourhood, and there I was, a saleswoman who had never handled a sale before. A lot of people came out to see this property. Most were just sightseers. Among the visitors that day, a couple arrived, perhaps in their sixties, and I showed them around and gave them a prepared pamphlet. They did not look like buyers — I judged them to be too casual in appearance. This was a big mistake on my part, and these folks decided to buy the property!

I learned a valuable lesson that day — to not judge people by their appearance. On the following Monday, I made certain to register as a real estate student to enable me to get the needed permit to sell real estate. Selling real estate became a successful career for me for many years.

Family Reunion

Although I had been able to trace my parents through the Red Cross after the war, staying in touch by mail since then had been difficult — but it did keep us connected.

My father and stepmother were living in Kiev in the Soviet Union (now Kyiv, Ukraine), and I learned that they had a child together. Their daughter, Sarina, was a pretty little girl who brought sunshine into their lives. Photos they sent of her helped me follow her development.

I decided it was time to see them. Once I started to investigate the possibility of a journey behind the "Iron Curtain," as the political barriers between the Soviet Union and the West was known at that time, I was informed that South Africa had no diplomatic ties with the country and that therefore travel visas were unobtainable. The only solution I could find was to arrange the entire journey through a travel agency in London, England.

Fortunately for me, my husband's work in aviation made flying to London possible; what was a problem for me was leaving my children for a short while. Bill's youngest sister, who was still single at the time and whom my children adored, offered to move in to take care of them while I was gone. They were in safe hands, so we decided that Bill would accompany me as far as London, and from there I would be on my own.

In 1963, I set off on this journey. I stayed in London with friends who helped me find a reputable travel agency that got to work on the required visas immediately. The agency pointed out that tourists to the Soviet Union were not permitted to stay with family and could only stay in hotels. I also learned that sightseeing in the Soviet Union could only be done in the company of a guide who would be assigned to me on arrival. It was a strange setup, but I had to accept the imposed restrictions. A room was booked for me at a hotel in Kiev, and when all arrangements for the trip, including the entry visa, were successfully concluded, I made my way to my destination, feeling somewhat overwhelmed.

Taking a train proved to be a practical solution. On the day of departure, the train left Victoria station in London direct to Brussels, Belgium. From this point, the train travelled through Germany. I could see Berlin's Brandenburg Gate at the border, symbolizing the division of the city, and my attention was caught by the stark difference between East and West Berlin. As the train made its journey through the eastern part, the city looked grey, dull, silent, almost eerie. When I had approached the western side earlier, it visibly pulsated with life — cars and people everywhere — a contrast impossible to ignore.

The next stop was Krakow, Poland, where I boarded the Trans-Siberian Railway. The formalities were daunting — there were hours of delays and endless red tape. Incidentally, I had second-class tickets, which guaranteed better seats everywhere in the world except in the Soviet Union. When I boarded and searched for my seat, I was told there was only one class for everyone, that all seats were alike. Once settled, I began paying attention to people around me. Some appeared to be daily commuters; others were peasants, carrying live chickens as hand luggage; some carried vegetables obviously for the market. It was a quiet, gloomy ride; no one engaged in conversation.

Close to where I was seated, a young woman was crying, wiping her eyes unsuccessfully with a small handkerchief. Turning, I offered her a few tissues I had. She took the tissues from me and a look of in-credulity appeared on her face. She fingered those tissues in wonder and stopped crying; from her body language, I understood she did not know what they were. Fortunately, I had a box of them in the tote I carried, which I gave to her. She thanked me profusely in Polish. This minor incident made me realize how different her country was from what I knew.

At the Soviet border, my passport was inspected once again for good measure. One of the authorities remarked with derision about the apartheid regime in my country, a remark I would hear many more times through my travels.

On arriving at my destination, Kiev, I was overcome with mixed emotions and fear. I longed and needed to be with my family, but instead I stayed at a hotel, where, perhaps, unseen eyes could keep all visitors under surveillance.

I finally saw my parents waiting for me — it was a dream come true and one of the happiest moments of my life. A tearful reunion followed, the culmination of years of never-ending hope and prayers. After all the misery we lived through, the impossible had happened — we were reunited and it was sheer bliss.

The hotel booked for me was an imposing building, obviously ancient. It had a spacious, well-appointed foyer, chandeliers and ori-ental carpets everywhere, including in my room, which was sumptu-ously furnished with large dark furniture.

At the check-in desk, I surrendered my passport. Later I was in-troduced to the guide assigned to me. She wasn't completely fluent in English, but she told me she was available if I wanted to tour the city museums or take photographs, and to let her know. She was cold and overly efficient, and I made a mental note to avoid her services as much as possible — besides, this was not a cultural visit for me, but a short, poignant week to spend with family I had not seen since 1944.

The hotel booking included breakfast, which, to my dismay, con-sisted of meat stews, borscht and other types of soup, plenty of sour cream, and the inevitable Russian tea in a fancy samovar. Asking for toast, I found myself entering into a serious and animated discussion with the waiter, whom I failed to convince that stews and soups first thing in the morning was not my choice breakfast. He left, presumably to the kitchen, and after a while returned triumphantly to present me with two thick slices of burnished toast (more roasted than toasted) that could have fed at least four more people. It was breakfast, nevertheless.

While waiting in the hotel's very busy foyer, a gentleman sitting close by began talking to me. He was American, from Chicago, Illinois, and a manufacturer of coats — in fact, most people in the foyer were US businesspeople, there to showcase, advertise and take orders for their merchandise. This man wanted to know all about my visit, and I told him as much as I could. After listening intently to my story, he handed me a catalogue of coats his company manufactured — a most impressive, beautiful selection — then stunned me by saying, "Choose any item you'd like for yourself, I will have it shipped to you on my return."

At first, I thought he was joking, but he assured me he wanted me to have whatever I chose. Touched, I thanked him profusely and let him know that I would be honoured to wear one of his beautiful coats. The coat of my choice, a faux-fur leopard print, was beautiful and elegant, with a quilted warm lining, and classy. I gave him my South African postal address, and we said our goodbyes, as he had business to attend, and I expected my father to arrive at any time.

After all these years, I still have the famous coat — it arrived shortly after my return — and had years of enjoyable wear out of it. In appreciation of his gift, we sent him two fluffy African motif blankets known to be the choice of tourists, and his family were delighted with our gift.

My father came to take me to their home, by bus. It was difficult not to notice the city's decaying roads. Houses along the way that had probably been beautiful now looked neglected, shabby. My family lived in a four-bedroom house, each bedroom divided by the government into a one-room domicile. The house itself had seen better days. Not only did my family live in one room but they shared a washroom with three other families. No water on tap, either — water had to be carried into their room for their daily needs. It was a basic way of life. Their cramped conditions seemed to be a common situation, not an isolated case; people were allotted domiciles based on availability at a time when the country was experiencing a serious housing shortage.

This was the first time I met my half-sister, who was now thirteen years old. Happy to be together, we never stopped talking as we shared experiences and tried to bridge the years of our separation. Sarina seemed to be enjoying herself and was affectionate with me.

My parents told me of their uncertainty when the war ended. Relieved and happy to leave the camp, they were not given a choice but were taken to Kiev, given a place to stay and were surviving on a small government pension. Looking around their room, I found it difficult to envisage three people who slept, ate, washed and lived in this tiny space. I heard their stories about the hardships they and so many others had endured. It was evident that theirs was a life lived in uncertainty and trepidation.

I was convinced that this was not the real Communism preached by Karl Marx, where everyone is treated equally. Far from it. There were huge divisions among the people. Those in government service had everything; the rest had nothing. What they did have was excellent theatre, ballet, opera and symphony, and admission was not expensive. Citizens (or comrades, as they were known) frequented almost every cultural event. I believe this uplifted their spirits, perhaps allowing them to escape the reality of their restricted lives.

I found it interesting to note that Communism did not allow religious worship; their magnificent Greek Orthodox churches were turned into museums, which all tourists were encouraged to visit.

During my stay, I grew aware of acute shortages of simple consumer goods. Some stores sold Czechoslovakian crystal to tourists and little else. Food stores had a limited selection of groceries. Fortunately, I had been primed, prior to embarking on this trip, to bring various consumer goods for which there was a ready market; my parents sold these items, which provided them with a small income, so badly needed. Their currency, the ruble, was worthless against the dollar. Later, after consulting my husband, we undertook to send my family a small amount of dollars on a monthly basis to help them cope with daily expenses.

The visit was just one week but meaningful. Although it was difficult to part from them, when the time came I was ready and eager to return to my family and the life I cherished.

Paperwork for this journey was supposed to include everything demanded by the various countries on the return trip. It did not work out that way. In Poland, I was unceremoniously taken off the train! The reason given — no visa. It was the stuff of nightmares. In the intense, sweltering heat of July, I had to make my way to the consulate. After copious red tape, excessive delays, plus many magical dollars, I was relieved to obtain the document allowing me to leave.

After that, the journey back was uneventful. In Belgium I got off the train and made my way to Paris, where I arranged to meet my friend Betty Bates. She and her family had lived in Israel in the same high-rise building Bill and I had years earlier. The two of us had made prior plans to spend a few days in Paris together. She booked us into a small, unremarkable hotel, which had an antiquated elevator, a narrow cage hand-operated by chains and ropes delivering passengers to the next floor. It was frightening at the start, but we soon got used to this mode of transport.

Betty lived in Luxembourg with her family and would often visit the nearby surrounding countries, France being one of them. She knew Paris well, and with her I got an insider's experience of the city, though I also made sure I saw the Louvre, world-famous enchanting buildings, cathedrals, famous shopping places. It was soon time to go back home, but we made wonderful memories, which I treasure.

Epilogue

Time, as we all know, has a habit of moving on.

Our sons received a good grounding and education. While they were growing up, South African law decreed that white males between the ages of seventeen and sixty-five serve a compulsory two years in the South African military. Conscientious objectors were punished with jail time. Therefore, each of our sons served in the military for the obligatory time. I disliked not having them home, but we nevertheless had to comply.

Once out of the army, one by one the boys found their niches. Our eldest, Laurence, decided to study for commercial degrees at Wits University; he got himself a few degrees and later he studied for and obtained a master's degree. At about the same time, he and his long-time sweetheart got engaged. Our second son, Mark, having privately earned his pilot's licence, remained in the South African Air Force, receiving pilot flying training there as well. He became adjutant to the head of the South African Air Force, a high-ranking pilot, before he decided to accept a position with one of the best-known world airlines. Our youngest son, William, was passionate about rowing at an early age and grew to be an accomplished rower, winner of many extraordinary rowing competitions in South Africa and abroad. He went into the commerce industry and had a successful career. He continues his amazing passion for rowing to this day.

When our sons realized they could not achieve their potential in South Africa, one by one they decided for reasons of their own to leave for North America in search of a more stable, better future.

After thirty-five years in the country, we were alone — just the two of us and our dog, with our children thousands of miles away. The idea of not being part of their and our future grandchildren's lives was too painful to contemplate. We decided to follow them. Our eldest son and his family were firmly established in Canada by this time and sponsored us. We applied to immigrate to Canada and were easily accepted.

In 1989, we sold our property, packed our belongings into a shipping container, said our goodbyes and took a trip that completely changed our lives as we knew it. It took time to find a suitable place that would be close enough to where our eldest son and family lived and also fulfill all our other needs. We chose Mississauga, Ontario. Both of us felt at home in Canada; we enjoyed our surroundings a lot and felt welcomed and accepted.

I wanted to continue the same work in Canada I had done for the last part of our life in South Africa — selling property, to which I was well suited. I took the four required courses needed to obtain a realtor's licence, which took a while, and earned my credentials, allowing me to work in real estate. My entrance into the industry was not crowned with immediate success; it took at least a couple of years to get to know in detail the geography of our chosen area.

In 2008, my beloved husband passed away, leaving a huge void in my life. We'd been married for fifty-seven years. Despite living alone now, I am able to live in total safety, go anywhere I need to be while enjoying the feeling of freedom and peace this country has given me. And thankfully, enjoying the benefits afforded to seniors.

It is mainly because Canada gives someone like me peace of mind and the ability to live life in safety that I decided to volunteer my time at a hospice nearby, to give back for all I've been given through the years. I am happy and proud to be Canadian.

Glossary

Antonescu, Ion (1882–1946) The prime minister of Romania from September 1940 to August 1944 and marshal of Romania from 1941. Antonescu allied his country with Nazi Germany, aiming to expand the territory of Romania, and his regime was responsible for the deaths of between 280,000 and 380,000 Jews from territory controlled by Romania and at least 12,000 Roma. Under his antisemitic, nationalistic and dictatorial regime, anti-Jewish measures were implemented; a brutal pogrom was instigated in the city of Iași, in which thousands of Jews were killed; and tens of thousands of Jews were murdered in other mass killings. Antonescu did not deport the entire Jewish population of the country but did sanction the deportation of Jews in the Romanian borderlands of Bessarabia and Bukovina, sending nearly two hundred thousand Jewish civilians to the Romanian-controlled territory of Transnistria, where the majority either died in captivity or were murdered. Ion Antonescu was executed for war crimes in 1946. *See also* Transnistria.

apartheid (Afrikaans; apartness) The South African policy of racial segregation that favoured the country's white minority and discriminated against non-whites. The policy was implemented in 1948 and instituted laws that controlled property ownership, employment, sexual relationships, education and voting rights of non-white citizens. The legislation supporting apartheid was repealed in 1991, though its social and economic effects are ongoing.

Atlit (detention centre) A detainee camp in British Mandate Palestine near the town of Atlit, established in the 1930s. The camp was surrounded by barbed wired and watchtowers and held thousands of Jewish immigrants who had come to Palestine without valid immigration documents. Immigrants were usually released only according to the monthly immigration quota. After the State of Israel was established in 1948, the camp was used as a military prison by Israel. It became a national monument in 1987 and is now a museum that documents the clandestine immigration of Jews to Palestine.

Brandenburg Gate The last remaining gate into Berlin. The gate was built between 1788 and 1791 and became one of the best-known symbols of the city. From 1961 to 1989, when Berlin was divided into West Berlin and East Berlin, the Brandenburg Gate, situated along the border between the two sections and closed to both sides, came to symbolize this division.

British Mandate Palestine (also Mandatory Palestine) The area of the Middle East under British rule from 1923 to 1948 comprising present-day Israel, Jordan, the West Bank and the Gaza Strip. The Mandate was established by the League of Nations after World War I and the collapse of the Ottoman Empire; the area was given to the British to administer until a Jewish national home could be established. During this time, Jewish immigration was severely restricted, and Jews and Arabs clashed with the British and each other as they struggled to realize their national interests. The Mandate ended on May 15, 1948, after the United Nations Partition Plan for Palestine was adopted and on the same day that the State of Israel was declared.

Haganah (Hebrew; The Defense) The Jewish paramilitary force in British Mandate Palestine that existed from 1920 to 1948 and later became the Israel Defense Forces. After World War II, there were branches of the Haganah in the displaced persons camps in Europe, and members helped coordinate illegal immigration to British Mandate Palestine.

hora An Israeli folk dance that is performed by a group in a circle and is traditionally danced on celebratory occasions.

International Red Cross (International Committee of the Red Cross, ICRC) A humanitarian organization founded in 1863 to protect the victims of war. During World War II, the Red Cross provided assistance to prisoners of war by distributing food parcels and monitoring the situation in prisoner-of-war (POW) camps and also provided medical attention to wounded soldiers and civilians. Today, in addition to the international body, the ICRC, there are national Red Cross and Red Crescent societies in almost every country in the world.

Internationale A left-wing anthem adopted by the socialist movement in the late nineteenth century. It was the de facto national anthem of the Soviet Union from 1922 until 1944 and is still sung by left-wing groups to this day. Originally in French, a Russian version was written in 1918.

Iron Curtain A term made famous by former British prime minister Winston Churchill in 1946 that described the political and ideological barrier maintained by the Soviet Union to isolate its dependent allies in Eastern and Central Europe from non-Communist Western Europe after World War II. The Communist governments behind the Iron Curtain exerted rigid control over the flow of information and people to and from the West until the collapse of Communism in 1989.

Iron Guard A military branch of the Legion of the Archangel Michael, a fascist political organization and party founded in Romania in 1927. Also known as the Legion or the Legionary Movement, the term Iron Guard came to encompass the entire organization, which was both nationalistic and extremely antisemitic in nature. The Iron Guard instigated violent pogroms against Jews with a goal to drive them out of Romania and grew in political influence and power between 1930 and 1941, ultimately becoming part of Ion Antonescu's government. This new joint regime, called the National Legionary State, ruled between September 1940 and January 1941. During this period, Jewish property was seized, Jews were deported from rural areas, foreign Jews were deported and anti-Jewish terror escalated. In January 1941, the Iron Guard movement was crushed when it attempted to overthrow Antonescu's dictatorial regime.

kibbutz (Hebrew; pl. kibbutzim) A collectively owned farm or settlement in Israel, democratically governed by its members.

King Carol II (1893–1953) King of Romania from 1930 to 1940. He became crown prince in 1914 after the death of his grand-uncle, King Carol I, but had to renounce his rights to the throne and go into exile because of his personal life and political views. King Carol II returned from exile in 1930 to take over from the regency that ruled for his young son, Michael, and slowly began to seize more power. In 1938, he declared a dictatorship. When Romania lost territory during World War II, the popular nationalist movements branded King Carol II a weak ruler, and he was forced to abdicate. In 1940, he went into exile, leaving the throne to his son, Michael.

Murafa A ghetto in the town of Murafa in the region of Transnistria, which was under the control of Romanian authorities. In the fall of 1941, a ghetto was established in "Old Murafa," the area of town where Jews lived. The open ghetto held 3,500 Jews who were deported from Romania and became very overcrowded. Hundreds of inhabitants of the ghetto died in a typhus epidemic in the winter of 1941. Jews in the Murafa ghetto were required to do forced labour on building sites and on farms. The ghetto had a Jewish council and a Jewish police force, which implemented the demands of the ghetto authorities. Welfare institutions such as a soup kitchen, hospital and orphanage were set up, which may have contributed to the relatively high survival rate in the ghetto. The Soviet army liberated the ghetto on March 19, 1944. *See also* Transnistria.

Shabbat (Hebrew; in Yiddish, Shabbes, Shabbos) The weekly day of rest beginning Friday at sunset and ending Saturday at nightfall, ushered in by the lighting of candles on Friday evening and the recitation of blessings over wine and challah (egg bread). A day of celebration as well as prayer, it is customary to eat three festive meals, attend synagogue services and refrain from doing any work or travelling.

shiva (Hebrew; seven) In Judaism, the seven-day mourning period that is observed after the funeral of a close relative.

Star of David (in Hebrew, *Magen David*) The six-pointed star that is the most recognizable symbol of Judaism. During World War II, Jews in Nazi-occupied areas were frequently forced to wear a badge or armband with the Star of David on it as an identifying mark of their lesser status and to single them out as targets for persecution.

Torah (in Hebrew, Sefer Torah) A scroll of parchment containing the text of the Torah, specifically the Five Books of Moses (the first books of the Hebrew Bible), the content of which is traditionally believed to have been revealed to Moses at Mount Sinai. The Torah scroll is handwritten by a trained scribe with ink and a quill and is covered with a decorative mantle or case and with silver or gold ornaments. The scroll is used for Torah readings and prayers in synagogues, where it is housed in a special ark and treated with great respect.

Transnistria A 40,000-square-kilometre strip of land between the Dniester and Bug rivers controlled by Romania from 1941 to 1944 that was used as a site to concentrate and persecute Jews. Previously part of Ukraine, the territory was conquered during the German and Romanian invasion of the Soviet Union. Romania administered this territory and deported nearly two hundred thousand Jews to the area, where they joined the remnants of the local Jewish population that had been destroyed during the invasion. Approximately 150 small, rudimentary ghettos and camps were created in Transnistria, and the majority of the Jews held there were killed or died of illness and starvation before the area was liberated in March 1944.

Photographs

Margalith's mother, Rachel (centre), with Margalith's paternal aunt, Gisele (right), and her sister, Dorica (in front). The name of the person on the left is not known. Rădăuţi, Romania, 1928.

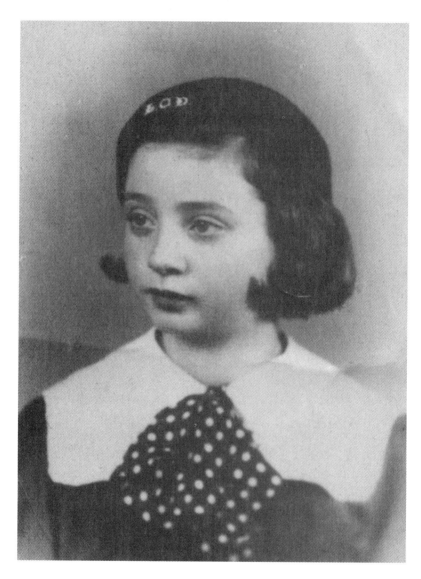

Dorica, circa 1935.

Margalith's father, Moritz, and her stepmother, Ethel, before the war. Edineți, Romania, date unknown.

1   2   3

4

1–3 The Hirsh family, who took care of Margalith after she was released from Transnistria. Chişinău, Romania (now in Moldova), 1944.

4 Margalith (left) with her uncle Seymour and aunt Gusty soon after arriving in British Mandate Palestine in 1945.

1 & 2 Margalith (right) with friends in Palestine. Circa 1945–1946.

3 Margalith (left) with a friend. Palestine, circa 1946.

4 Margalith. Palestine, circa 1946.

1 Margalith during her army service. Israel, circa 1948–1950.

2 & 3 Margalith (right) with friends during their army service. Israel, circa 1948–1950.

Margalith and her husband, Bill, who accompanied her partway on her travels to the Soviet Union to reunite with her family. Luxembourg, 1963.

1 Margalith and Bill with their sons Mark (left) and William (right). Johannesburg, South Africa, circa 1964.

2 Margalith's husband, Bill, with their three children, William (left), Mark (centre, back) and Laurence (right), on holiday in the Cape Province. South Africa, 1966.

1   Margalith with her father, Moritz, and stepmother, Ethel, when Margalith visited
    them in Israel in the 1970s.
2   Moritz and Ethel. Israel, 1970s.
3   Margalith (front) with her family. From left to right: Aunt Gisele, Moritz, Marga-
    lith, Ethel, Uncle Bernard and Bernard's sister, Rosa. Israel, 1970s.

1 Margalith's sons William (left) and Laurence (right) meeting their grandfather Moritz for the first time. Montreal, Quebec, 1987.

2 From left to right: Margalith's daughter-in-law Joyce, Margalith's aunt Gisele, Moritz, Margalith's uncle Bernard, and her son William. Montreal, 1987.

1 Margalith and Bill. Mississauga, Ontario, 1993.
2 Bill and Margalith. Niagara Falls, Ontario, 1995.
3 The Esterhuizen family celebrating Bill's 80th birthday. From left to right (in back): Margalith's son William, her daughter-in-law Kira, her son Mark, her granddaughter Rebecca, her granddaughter Irene, her daughter-in-law Hester and her son Laurence. Standing in front, left to right: Margalith's grandson Max, her daughter-in-law Joyce, her granddaughter Morgan, Margalith and Bill. Niagara region, 2003.

1 Margalith with her granddaughters Rebecca and Elisabeth. Victoria, BC, 2010.
2 Margalith with her granddaughter Irene. Caledon, Ontario, 2012.
3 Margalith's grandchildren Morgan and Max. Virginia, US, 2018.

Margalith in her backyard. Caledon, Ontario, 2020.

Index

to and return from, 59–61, 64;
parents' postwar relocation to,
42, 63
Kishinev, Romania (later Chişinău,
Moldova), xv–xvi, xxvii, 38
lice infestations, 36
Lipcani, Romania, 14
Lod Airport (later Ben Gurion),
51–52
Luxair airline, 55
Maimon, Gusty (aunt by marriage),
44
Maimon, Seymour (maternal
uncle), 43, 47
Maimon grandparents, xxviii, 5–6, 7
Mendelsohn, Ezra, xx
"Minorities Treaties" (Paris, 1919),
xviii
Mississauga, Ontario, 66
Moghilev-Podolsk (now Mohyliv-
Podilskyi, Ukraine), xxiii, xxiv,
xxv, 33
Molotov-Ribbentrop Pact, xix
Mozambique, travels in, 56
Murafa ghetto (Transnistria), xxiv–
xxv, xxvi, xxvii, 33, 34–36
National Legionary State, xix
Negev Desert, 49, 51
Odessa, mass murder of Jews in, xxi
Palestine: Atlit detention camp,
41–43; Ayanot agricultural col-
lege, 44–46; British in, 9–10, 42,
43–44; Haganah, 42; Hebrew
language studies, 41; Herscovici
family attempted immigration
to, 9–10; night school studies in,

47–48; repatriation and passage
to, xxvii, 36–39
Paris visit, 64
Rădăuţi, Romania, xvi, xvii, 4–5
real estate career, 58, 66
Romania: army of, xix–xx, xxi,
19–20; constitution of 1923,
xviii; Nazi alignment in, xviii,
xix, xxi, 19–20, 21; postwar
Jewish emigration from, xxviii;
pre-war Jewish population in,
xv, xvii; pre-war life in, xv, 3–4;
Soviet invasion and occupation
of, xviii–xix, 17–19; stages of
the Holocaust in, xx–xxii. See
also antisemitism; Transnistria
Governate
Romanianization, xvii–xviii
Rosen, Sarah, xxiv–xxv, xxvi
sabras, 49
shidduch, 4
South Africa: apartheid in, 55, 56,
57, 61; moving to, 54; Nestlé,
employment with, 58; raising
a family in, 55–56; real estate
career in, 58
Soviet military, xix, xxvii, 17–19
Soviet Union. See Kiev, Soviet
Union (now Kyiv, Ukraine)
Springs, South Africa, 53
Tel Aviv, 44, 51–52
Tiraspol Agreement of August 20,
1941, xxii
Transnistria Governate: camp and
ghetto conditions in, xxiii–xxiv,
xxv–xxvii; death toll in, xxviii;

The Azrieli Foundation was established in 1989 to realize and extend the philanthropic vision of David J. Azrieli, C.M., C.Q., M.Arch. The Foundation's mission is to support a wide spectrum of initiatives in education and research. The Azrieli Foundation is an active supporter of programs in the fields of education, the education of architects, scientific and medical research, and the arts. The Azrieli Foundation's many initiatives include: the Holocaust Survivor Memoirs Program, which collects, preserves, publishes and distributes the written memoirs of survivors in Canada; the Azrieli Institute for Educational Empowerment, an innovative program successfully working to keep at-risk youth in school; the Azrieli Fellows Program, which promotes academic excellence and leadership on the graduate level at Israeli universities; the Azrieli Music Project, which celebrates and fosters the creation of high-quality new Jewish orchestral music; and the Azrieli Neurodevelopmental Research Program, which supports advanced research on neurodevelopmental disorders, particularly Fragile X and Autism Spectrum Disorders.